Hands-On Generative Adversarial Networks with Keras

Your guide to implementing next-generation generative adversarial networks

Rafael Valle

BIRMINGHAM - MUMBAI

Hands-On Generative Adversarial Networks with Keras

Commissioning Editor: Sunith Shetty
Acquisition Editor: Yogesh Deokar
Content Development Editor: Athikho Sapuni Rishana
Technical Editor: Kushal Shingote
Copy Editor: Safis Editing
Project Coordinator: Kirti Pisat
Proofreader: Safis Editing
Indexer: Tejal Daruwale Soni
Graphics: Jisha Chirayil
Production Coordinator: Nilesh Mohite

First published: May 2019

Production reference: 1020519

Published by Packt Publishing Ltd.
Livery Place
35 Livery Street
Birmingham
B3 2PB, UK.

ISBN 978-1-78953-820-5

www.packtpub.com

`mapt.io`

Mapt is an online digital library that gives you full access to over 5,000 books and videos, as well as industry leading tools to help you plan your personal development and advance your career. For more information, please visit our website.

Why subscribe?

- Spend less time learning and more time coding with practical eBooks and Videos from over 4,000 industry professionals

- Improve your learning with Skill Plans built especially for you

- Get a free eBook or video every month

- Mapt is fully searchable

- Copy and paste, print, and bookmark content

Packt.com

Did you know that Packt offers eBook versions of every book published, with PDF and ePub files available? You can upgrade to the eBook version at `www.packt.com` and as a print book customer, you are entitled to a discount on the eBook copy. Get in touch with us at `customercare@packtpub.com` for more details.

At `www.packt.com`, you can also read a collection of free technical articles, sign up for a range of free newsletters, and receive exclusive discounts and offers on Packt books and eBooks.

Foreword

I have known and worked with Rafael for about two years. Rafael is an expert in machine learning and deep learning in various tasks, and is particularly well known for his work in speech synthesis. In this book, Rafael will take you into a new world full of interesting things a **Deep Neural Network (DNN)** can do.

For those who are not familiar with DNNs, this book explains the basics and helps you set up the environment to train your first neural network. It then goes on to introduce a very popular class of DNNs, called **Generative Adversarial Networks (GANs)**. This book goes through the principal ideas behind GANs, how to train and evaluate your first GANs, and the problems you might encounter while training them. To improve your results and stabilize your training procedure, you might find several tricks listed in the book to be very useful. Finally, the book shows several applications of GANs in different areas, including computer vision, natural language processing, and speech processing. Experience the fun and joy of turning simple lines of code into tangible images or audio.

The book approaches the concepts of GANs in both a mathematical and an intuitive way. After you have completed the book, you will be familiar with the GANs that are commonly used nowadays, as well as their different use cases and their potential impacts. You will also get to know the mechanism of training GANs, the current limitations of GANs, and the future of GANs. Most importantly, the book provides extensive hands-on examples to really help you implement everything from the ground up, so you can learn from your own experiences.

Get ready for the journey to see the fascinating world built by GANs.

Ting-Chun Wang

Senior Research Scientist, NVIDIA

Contributors

About the author

Rafael Valle is a research scientist at NVIDIA focusing on audio applications. He has years of experience developing high-performance machine learning models for data/audio analysis, synthesis and machine improvisation with formal specifications.

Dr. Valle was the first to generate speech samples from scratch with GANs and to show that simple yet efficient techniques can be used to identify GAN samples. He holds an Interdisciplinary Ph.D. in Machine Listening and Improvisation from UC Berkeley, a Master's degree in Computer Music from the MH-Stuttgart in Germany and a Bachelor's degree in Orchestral Conducting from UFRJ in Brazil.

About the reviewer

Sujit Pal is a Technology Research Director at Elsevier Labs, an advanced technology group within the Reed-Elsevier Group of companies. His areas of interest include Semantic Search, Natural Language Processing, Machine Learning and Deep Learning. At Elsevier, he has worked on several machine learning initiatives involving large image and text corpora, and other initiatives round recommendation systems and knowledge graph development. He has co-authored a book on Deep Learning with Antonio Gulli and writes about technology on his blog Salmon Run.

Packt is searching for authors like you

If you're interested in becoming an author for Packt, please visit `authors.packtpub.com` and apply today. We have worked with thousands of developers and tech professionals, just like you, to help them share their insight with the global tech community. You can make a general application, apply for a specific hot topic that we are recruiting an author for, or submit your own idea.

Table of Contents

Preface

Generative Adversarial Networks (GANs) have revolutionized the fields of machine learning and deep learning. This book will be your first step towards understanding GAN architectures and tackling the challenges involved in training them.

This book opens with an introduction to deep learning and generative models, and their applications in artificial intelligence (AI). You will then learn how to build, evaluate, and improve your first GAN with the help of easy-to-follow examples. The next few chapters will guide you through training a GAN model to produce and improve high-resolution images. You will also learn how to implement conditional GANs that give you the ability to control characteristics of GAN outputs. You will build on your knowledge further by exploring a new training methodology for progressive growing of GANs. Moving on, you'll gain insights into state-of-the-art models in image synthesis, speech enhancement, and natural language generation using GANs. In addition to this, you'll be able to identify GAN samples with TequilaGAN.

By the end of this book, you will be well-versed with the latest advancements in the GAN framework using various examples, and datasets and you will have the skills you need to implement GAN architectures for several tasks and domains, including computer vision, natural language processing (NLP), and audio processing.

Who this book is for

This book is for machine learning practitioners, deep learning researchers, and AI enthusiasts who are looking for a perfect mix of theory and hands-on content in order to implement GANs using Keras. A working knowledge of Python is expected.

What this book covers

Chapter 1, *Deep Learning Basics and Environment Setup*, contains essential knowledge for building and training deep learning models, including GANs. In this chapter, you will also learn how to set up your deep learning Python and Keras environments for the upcoming projects. Finally, you will learn about the importance of using GPUs in deep learning and how to choose the platform that best suits you.

Chapter 2, *Introduction to Generative Models*, covers the basics of generative models, including GANs, variational autoencoders, autoregressive models and reversible flow models. You will learn about state-of-the-art applications that use GANs. You will learn the building blocks of GANs, along with their strengths and limitations.

Chapter 3, *Implementing Your First GAN*, explains the basics of implementing and training a GAN for image synthesis. You will learn how to implement the generator and discriminator in a GAN. You will learn how to implement your loss function and how to use it to train your GAN models. You will learn how to visualize the samples from your first GAN. We will focus on the well-known CIFAR10 dataset, with 60,000 32 by 32 color images in 10 classes, naturally including dogs and cats.

Chapter 4, *Evaluating Your First GAN*, covers how to use quantitative and qualitative methods to evaluate the quality and variety of the GAN samples you produced in the previous chapter. You will learn about the challenges involved in evaluating GAN samples. You will learn how to implement metrics for image quality. You will learn about using the birthday paradox to evaluate sample variety.

Chapter 5, *Improving Your First GAN*, explains the main challenges in training and understanding GANs, and how to solve them. You will learn about vanishing gradients, mode collapse, training instability, and other challenges. You will learn how to solve the challenges that arise when training GANs by using tricks of the trade and improving your GAN architecture and your loss function. You will learn about multiple deep learning model architectures that have been successful with the GAN framework. Furthermore, you will learn how to improve your first GAN by implementing new loss functions and algorithms. We will continue to focus on the CIFAR-10 dataset.

Chapter 6, *Synthesizing and Manipulating Images with GANs*, explains how to implement pix2pixHD: a method for high-resolution (such as 2048 x 1024) photo-realistic image-to-image translation. It can be used to turn semantic label maps into photo-realistic images or to synthesize portraits from face label maps. We will use the Cityscapes dataset, which focuses on a semantic understanding of urban street scenes.

Chapter 7, *Progressive Growing of GANs*, explains how to implement the progressive growing of GANs framework: a new training methodology in which the generator and discriminator are trained progressively. Starting from a low resolution, we will add new layers that model increasingly fine details as training progresses. This speeds up the training process and stabilizes it, allowing us to produce images of unprecedented quality. We will focus on the CelebFaces Attributes Dataset (CelebA): a face attributes dataset with over 200,000 celebrity images.

Chapter 8, *Natural Language Generation with GANs*, covers the implementation of adversarial generation of natural language: a model capable of generating sentences multiple languages from context-free and probabilistic context-free grammars. You will learn how to implement a model that generates sequences character by character and a model that generates sentences word by word. We will focus on the Google 1-billion-word dataset.

Chapter 9, *Text-To-Image Synthesis with GANs*, explains how to implement generative adversarial text to image synthesis: a model that generates plausible images from detailed text descriptions. You will learn about matching-aware discriminators, interpolations in embedding space and vector arithmetic. We will focus on the Oxford-102 Flowers dataset.

Chapter 10, *Speech Enhancement with GANs*, covers the implementation of a speech enhancement GAN: a framework for audio denoising and speech enhancement using GANs. You will learn how to train the model with multiple speakers and noise conditions. You will learn how to evaluate the model qualitatively and quantitatively. We will focus on the WSJ dataset and a noise dataset.

Chapter 11, *TequilaGAN: Identifying GAN Samples*, explains how to implement TequilaGAN. You will learn how to identify the underlying characteristics of GAN data and how to identify data to differentiate real data from fake data. You will implement strategies to easily identify fake samples that have been generated with the GAN framework. One strategy is based on the statistical analysis and comparison of raw pixel values and features extracted from them. The other strategy learns formal specifications from real data and shows that fake samples violate the specifications of the real data. We focus on the MNIST dataset of handwritten images, CIFAR-10, and a dataset of Bach Chorales.

Chapter 12, *What's Next in GANs?*, covers recent advances and open questions that relate to GANs. We start with a summary of this book and what it has covered, from the simplest to the state-of-the-art GANs. Then we address important open questions related to GANs. We also consider the artistic use of GANs in the visual and sonic arts. Finally, we take a look at new and yet-to-be-explored domains with GANs.

To get the most out of this book

This book will give you an overview of data analysis in Python. This will take you through the main libraries of Python's data science stack. It will explain how to use various Python tools to analyze, visualize, and process data effectively and you will learn about the importance of using GPUs in deep learning. The reader must have software and hardware experience in Python development.

Download the example code files

You can download the example code files for this book from your account at
`www.packt.com`. If you purchased this book elsewhere, you can visit
`www.packt.com/support` and register to have the files emailed directly to you.

You can download the code files by following these steps:

1. Log in or register at `www.packt.com`.
2. Select the **SUPPORT** tab.
3. Click on **Code Downloads & Errata**.
4. Enter the name of the book in the **Search** box and follow the onscreen
   instructions.

Once the file is downloaded, please make sure that you unzip or extract the folder using the
latest version of:

- WinRAR/7-Zip for Windows
- Zipeg/iZip/UnRarX for Mac
- 7-Zip/PeaZip for Linux

The code bundle for the book is also hosted on GitHub
at `https://github.com/PacktPublishing/Hands-On-Generative-Adversarial-Networks-with-Keras`. In case there's an update to the code, it will be updated on the existing GitHub
repository.

We also have other code bundles from our rich catalog of books and videos available
at `https://github.com/PacktPublishing/`. Check them out!

Download the color images

We also provide a PDF file that has color images of the screenshots/diagrams used in this
book. You can download it here: `https://www.packtpub.com/sites/default/files/downloads/9781789538205_ColorImages.pdf`.

Conventions used

There are a number of text conventions used throughout this book.

`CodeInText`: Indicates code words in text, database table names, folder names, filenames, file extensions, pathnames, dummy URLs, user input, and Twitter handles. Here is an example: "We are going to update all Anaconda packages using the `conda` command."

A block of code is set as follows:

```
import numpy as np
from keras.datasets import mnist
from keras.models import Sequential
from keras.utils import np_utils
from keras.optimizers import SGD
from keras.layers.core import Dense,Activation
```

Any command-line input or output is written as follows:

```
pip install keras
```

 Warnings or important notes appear like this.

 Tips and tricks appear like this.

Get in touch

Feedback from our readers is always welcome.

General feedback: If you have questions about any aspect of this book, mention the book title in the subject of your message and email us at customercare@packtpub.com.

Errata: Although we have taken every care to ensure the accuracy of our content, mistakes do happen. If you have found a mistake in this book, we would be grateful if you would report this to us. Please visit www.packt.com/submit-errata, selecting your book, clicking on the Errata Submission Form link, and entering the details.

Piracy: If you come across any illegal copies of our works in any form on the Internet, we would be grateful if you would provide us with the location address or website name. Please contact us at copyright@packt.com with a link to the material.

If you are interested in becoming an author: If there is a topic that you have expertise in and you are interested in either writing or contributing to a book, please visit authors.packtpub.com.

Reviews

Please leave a review. Once you have read and used this book, why not leave a review on the site that you purchased it from? Potential readers can then see and use your unbiased opinion to make purchase decisions, we at Packt can understand what you think about our products, and our authors can see your feedback on their book. Thank you!

For more information about Packt, please visit packt.com.

Section 1: Introduction and Environment Setup

This section features an introduction to the basics of deep learning, how to set up a deep learning environment with Python and Keras, and how to go about acquiring data. You will also benefit from an introduction to generative models, including **Generative Adversarial Networks (GANs)**, **Variational Autoencoders (VAEs)**, and **Normalizing Flow (NF)**.

The following chapters will be covered in this section:

- Chapter 1, *Deep Learning Basics and Environment Setup*
- Chapter 2, *Introduction to Generative Models*

1
Deep Learning Basics and Environment Setup

In this chapter, we offer you essential knowledge for building and training deep learning models, including **Generative Adversarial Networks (GANs)**. We are going to explain the basics of deep learning, starting with a simple example of a learning algorithm based on linear regression. We will also provide instructions on how to set up a deep learning programming environment using Python and Keras. We will also talk about the importance of computing power in deep learning; we are going to describe guidelines to fully take advantage of NVIDIA GPUs by maximizing the memory footprint, enabling the **CUDA Deep Neural Network library (cuDNN)**, and eventually using distributed training setups with multiple GPUs. Finally, in addition to installing the libraries that will be necessary for upcoming projects in this book, you will test your installation by building, from scratch, a simple and efficient **Artificial Neural Network (ANN)** that will learn from data how to classify images of handwritten digits.

The following major topics will be covered in this chapter:

- Deep learning basics
- Deep learning environment setup
- The deep learning environment test

Deep learning basics

Deep learning is a subset of machine learning, which is a field of artificial intelligence that uses mathematics and computers to learn from data and map it from some input to some output. Loosely speaking, a map or a model is a function with parameters that maps the input to an output. Learning the map, also known as mode, occurs by updating the parameters of the map such that some expected empirical loss is minimized. The empirical loss is a measure of distance between the values predicted by the model and the target values given the empirical data.

Notice that this learning setup is extremely powerful because it does not require having an explicit understanding of the rules that define the map. An interesting aspect of this setup is that it does not guarantee that you will learn the exact map that maps the input to the output, but some other maps, as expected, predict the correct output.

This learning setup, however, does not come without a price: some deep learning methods require large amounts of data, specially when compared with methods that rely on feature engineering. Fortunately, there is a large availability of free data, specially unlabeled, in many domains.

Meanwhile, the term deep learning refers to the use of multiple layers in an ANN to form a deep chain of functions. The term ANN suggests that such models informally draw inspiration from theoretical models of how learning could happen in the brain. ANNs, also referred to as deep neural networks, are the main class of models considered in this book.

Artificial Neural Networks (ANNs)

Despite its recent success in many applications, deep learning is not new and according to Ian Goodfellow, Yoshua Bengio, and Aaron Courville, there have been three eras:

- Cybernetics between the 1940s and the 1960s
- Connectionism between the 1980s and the 1990s
- The current deep learning renaissance beginning in 2006

Mathematically speaking, a neural network is a graph consisting of non-linear equations whose parameters can be estimated using methods such as stochastic gradient descent and backpropagation. We will introduce ANNs step by step, starting with linear and logistic regression.

Linear regression is used to estimate the parameters of a model to describe the relationship between an output variable and the given input variables. It can be mathematically described as a weighted sum of input variables:

$$f(x) = z = \mathbf{w}^T\mathbf{x} + b$$

Here, the weight, w, and inputs, X, are vectors in $\mathbb{R}^d$; in other words, they are real-valued vectors with d dimensions, b as a scalar bias term, and z as a scalar term that represents the valuation of the f function at the input x . In ANNs, the output of a single neuron without non-linearities is similar to the output of the linear model described in the preceding linear regression equation and the following diagram:

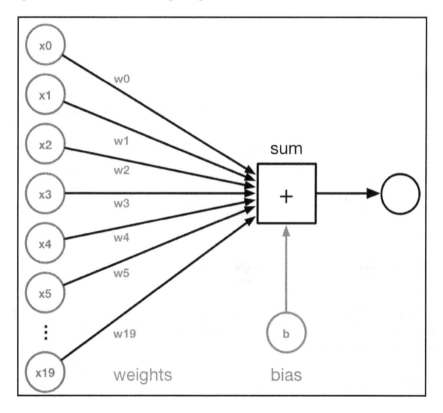

Logistic regression is a special version of regression where a specific non-linear function, the `sigmoid` function, is applied to the output of the linear model in the earlier linear regression equation:

$$g(z) = \frac{1}{1 + \exp^{-(z)}}$$

The In ANNs, the non-linear model described in the logistic regression equation is similar to the output of a single neuron with a sigmoid non-linearity in the following diagram:

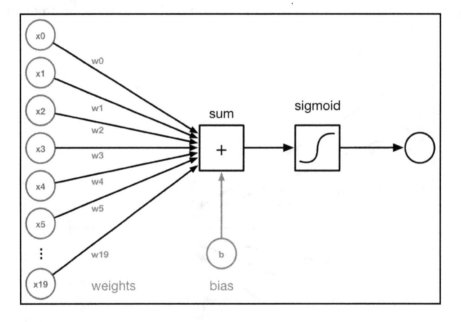

A combination of such neurons defines a hidden layer in a neural network, and the neural networks are organized as a chain of layers. The output of a hidden layer is described by the following equation and diagram:

$$\mathbf{h}^{(l)} = g^{(l)}\left(\mathbf{w}^{(l)} \cdot \mathbf{x} + b^{(l)}\right)$$

Here, the weight, $\mathbf{w}^{(l)}$, and the input, $\mathbf{x}$, are vectors in R^d, $b^{(l)}$ is a scalar bias term, $\mathbf{h}^{(l)}$ is a vector, and g is a non-linearity:

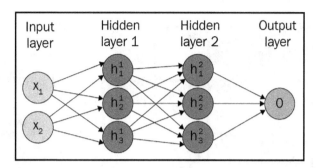

The preceding diagram depicts a fully connected neural network with two inputs, two hidden layers with three nodes each, and one output node.

In general, neural networks have a chain-like structure that is easy to visualize in equation form or as a graph, as the previous diagram confirms. For example, consider the f and g functions that are used in the $y = g(f(x))$ model. In this simple model of a neural network, the input x is used to produce the output $f(x)$; the output of $f(x)$ is used as the input of $g(f(x))$ that finally produces y.

In this simple model, the function f is considered to be the first hidden layer and the function g is considered to be the second hidden layer. These layers are called **hidden** because, unlike the input and the output values of the model that are known a priori, their values are not known.

In each layer, the network is learning features or projections of the data that are useful for the task at hand. For example, in computer vision, there is evidence that the layers of the network closer to the input can learn filters that are associated with basic shapes, whereas in the layers closer to the output the network might learn filters that are closer to images.

The following figure taken from the paper *Visualizing and Understanding Convolutional Networks* by Zeiler et Fergus, provides a visualization of the filters on the first convolution layer of a trained AlexNet:

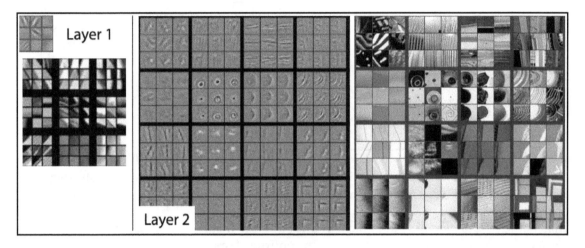

 For a thorough introduction to the topic of neural network visualization, refer to Stanford's class on *Convolutional Networks for Visual Recognition*.

The parameter estimation

The output of each layer on the network is dependent on the parameters of the model estimated by training the neural network to minimize the loss with respect to the weights, $L(w)$, as we described earlier. This is a general principle in machine learning, in which a learning procedure, for example backpropagation, uses the gradients of the error of a model to update its parameters to minimize the error. Consider estimating the parameters of a linear regression model such that the output of the model minimizes the **mean squared error** (**MSE**). Mathematically speaking, the point-wise error between the $w^T x$ predictions and the y target value is computed as follows:

$$e = y - w^T x,$$

The MSE is computed as follows:

$$L(w) = MSE(w) = \frac{1}{n}e^T e,$$

where $e^T e$ presents the sum of the squared errors (SSE) and $\frac{1}{n}$ normalizes the SSE with the number of samples to reach the mean squared error (MSE).

In the case of linear regression, the problem is convex and the MSE has the simple closed solution given in the following equation:

$$w = (X^T X)X^{-1}y$$

Here, w is the coefficient of the linear model, X refers to matrices with the observations and their respective features, and y is the response value associated with each observation. Note that this closed form solution requires the X matrix to be invertible and, hence, to have a determinant larger than 0.

In the case of models where a closed solution to the loss does not exist, we can estimate the parameters that minimize the MSE by computing the partial derivative of each weight with respect to the MSE loss, L, and using the negative of that value, scaled by a learning rate, α, to update the w parameters of the model being evaluated:

$$w := w - \alpha \frac{d}{d_w}L(w)$$

A model in which many of the coefficients in w are 0 is said to be sparse. Given the large number of parameters or coefficients in deep learning models, producing models that are sparse is valuable because it can reduce computation requirements and produce models with faster inference.

Backpropagation

The backpropagation algorithm is a special case of reverse-mode automatic differentiation. In its basic modern version, the backpropagation algorithm has become the standard for training neural networks, possibly due to its underlying simplicity and relative power.

Inspired by the work of Donal Hebb and the so-called Hebb rule, Rosenblatt developed the idea of a perceptron that was based on the formation and changes of synapses between neurons, where the output of a neuron will be modeled as a weighted sum based on its incoming signals. This weighted sum is similar to what we described in the equation(3) in this chapter.

The basic idea of backpropagation is as follows: to define an error function and reiteratively compute the gradients of the loss with respect to the model weights and perform gradient descent and weight updates that are optimal for minimizing the error function given the current data and model weights. From a perspective of calculus, backpropagation is an algorithm that efficiently computes the chain rule with a specific order of operations.

The data and the error function are extremely important factors of the learning procedure. For example, consider a classifier that is trained to identify single handwritten digits. For training the model, suppose we will use the MNIST dataset, (`http://yann.lecun.com/exdb/mnist/`) which is comprises 28 by 28 monochromatic images of single handwritten white digits on a black canvas, such as the ones in following figure. Ideally, we want the model to predict 1 whenever the image looks such as a 1, 2 whenever it looks such as a 2, and so on:

Note that backpropagation does not define what aspects of the images should be considered, nor does it provide guarantees that the classifier will not memorize the data or that it will get generalize to unseen examples. A model trained with such data will fail if the colors are inverted, for instance, black digits on a white canvas. Naturally, one way to fix this issue will be to augment the data to include images with any foreground and background color combination. This example illustrates the importance of the training data and the objective function being used.

Loss functions

A `loss` function, also known as a `cost` function, is a function that maps an event or values of one or more variables onto a real number intuitively representing some cost associated with the event. We will cover the following three loss functions in this chapter:

- L1 Loss
- L2 Loss
- Categorical Crossentropy Loss

L1 loss

The L1 loss function, also known as the mean absolute error, measures the average point-wise difference between the model prediction, $f(x_i)$, and the target value, y_i. The partial derivative is equal to 1 when the model prediction is larger than the target value, and equal to -1 when the prediction is smaller than the target error. This property of the L1 loss function can be used to circumvent problems that might arise when learning from noisy labels:

$$L_1 = \frac{1}{n} \sum_{i=1}^{n} \mid y_i - f(x_i) \mid$$

L2 loss

The L2 loss function, also known as MSE, measures the average point-wise squared difference between the prediction, $f(x_i)$, and the target value, y_i. Compared to the L1 loss function, the L2 loss function penalizes larger errors:

$$L_2 = \frac{1}{n} \sum_{i=1}^{n} (y_i - f(x_i))^2$$

Categorical crossentropy loss

The categorical crossentropy loss function measures the weighted divergence between targets, t, and predictions, p, where i denotes the data point, and j denotes the class. For single label classification problems, the t targets operate as an indicator variable and the loss is reduced to $\log p_{i,j}$:

$$Li = -\sum_{j} t_{i,j} \log p_{i,j}$$

Non-linearities

ANNs are normally non-linear models that use different types of non-linearities. The most commonly used are as follows:

- `sigmoid`
- `Tanh`
- `ReLU`

Sigmoid

The sigmoid non-linearity has an *S* shape and maps the input domain to an output range between [0, 1]. This characteristic of sigmoid makes it suitable for estimating probabilities, which are also in the [0, 1] range. The gradient of sigmoid is larger at its center, 0.0, and the gradients quickly vanish as the domain moves away from 0.0:

$$f(x) = \sigma(x) = \frac{1}{1 + e^x}$$

Tanh

The Tanh non-linearity has an *S* shape that is similar to the sigmoid non-linearity, but maps the input domain to an output range between [-1, 1]. In the same way as sigmoid, the gradient of Tanh is larger at its center, 0.0, but the gradient at the center is larger for the Tanh non-linearity, hence the derivatives are steeper and the gradient is stronger:

$$f(x) = tanh(x) = \frac{(e^x - e^{-x})}{(e^x + e^{-x})}$$

ReLU

The ReLU non-linearity is a piecewise linear function with a non-linearity introduced by rectification. Unlike the sigmoid and Tanh non-linearities that have continuous gradients, the gradients of ReLU have two values only: 0 for values smaller than 0, and 1 for values larger than 0. Hence, the gradients of ReLU are sparse. Although the gradient of ReLU at 0 is undefined, common practice sets it to 0. There are variations to the ReLU non-linearity including the ELU and the Leaky RELU. Compared to sigmoid and Tanh, the derivative of ReLU is faster to compute and induces sparsity in models:

$$f(x) = \begin{cases} 0 & \text{for } x < 0 \\ x & \text{otherwise} \end{cases}$$

A fully connected layer

Feedforward neural networks have this name because the flow of information being evaluated by the neural network starts at the input x, flows all the way through the hidden layers, and finally reaches the output y. Note that the output of each layer does flow back to itself. In some models there are residual connections in which the input of the layer is added or concatenated to the output of the layer itself. In the following figure, we provide a visualization in which the input of Layer 2, Out 1, is concatenated with the output of Layer 2:

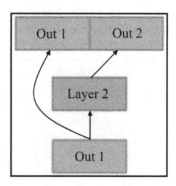

The convolution layer

Convolutional Neural Networks (CNNs) are neural networks that learn filters, tensors in R^d, which are convolved with the data. In the image domain, a filter is usually square and with small sizes ranging from 3 x 3 to 9 x 9 in pixel size. The convolution operation can be interpreted as sliding a filter over the data and, for each position, applying a dot product between the filter and the data at that position. The following diagram shows an intermediary step of convolution with stride **1** where the kernel in green is convolved with the first area in the data, represented by the red grid:

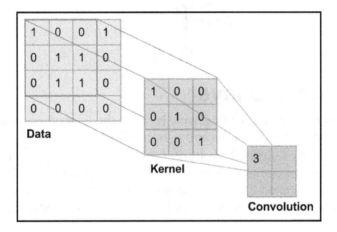

A special characteristic of CNNs is that the weights of the filters are learned. For example, if the task at hand is classifying monochromatic handwritten digits from the MNIST dataset, the ANN might learn filters that look similar to vertical, horizontal, and diagonal lines.

> For more information on CNNs and convolution arithmetic, we refer the reader to the book *Deep Learning* by Ian Goodfellow et al., and the excellent *A Guide to Convolution Arithmetic for Deep Learning* by Vincent Dumoulin and Francisco Visin.

The max pooling layer

The max pooling layer is a common non-linear filter in computer vision applications. Given an n by m window, it consists of choosing the largest value in that window. The max pooling layers reduces the dimensionality of the data, potentially preventing overfitting and reducing computational cost. Given that within the window the max pooling layer takes the largest value in the window, disregarding spatial information, the max pooling layers can be used to learn the representations that are locally invariant to translation:

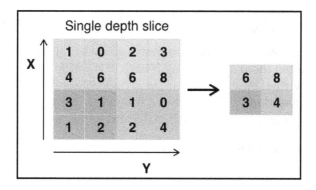

Deep learning environment setup

In this section, we will provide instructions on how to set up a Python deep learning programming environment that will be used throughout the book. We will start with Anaconda, which makes package management and deployment easy, and NVIDIA's CUDA Toolkit and cuDNN, which make training and inference in deep learning models quick. There are several compute cloud services, like Amazon Web Services (AWS), that provide ready to use deep learning environments with NVIDIA GPUs.

Installing Anaconda and Python

Anaconda is a free and open source efficient distribution that provides easy package management and deployment for the programming languages R and Python. Anaconda focuses on data science and deep learning applications and provides over 6 million users with hundreds of packages and support for Windows, Linux, and macOS.

Installing Anaconda is easy and simply requires downloading the installation wizard for a target Python version. We are going to download Anaconda's installation wizard for Python 3.5. The installation wizard can be downloaded on Anaconda's website at https:// www.anaconda.com/download/.

After following the wizard instructions and installing Anaconda, we are going to update all Anaconda packages using the conda command. To do so, open Anaconda's **Command-Line Interface (CLI)** and type the following commands:

```
conda update conda
conda update -all
```

Setting up a virtual environment in Anaconda

A virtual environment allows us to have different versions of libraries and executables, avoiding conflicts between them and making it easy to develop multiple projects at the same time. Creating a virtual environment in Anaconda is easy and only requires executing a single command on Anaconda's CLI. With the following command, we are going to `create` a virtual environment running Python 3.5 and name it `deeplearning`:

```
conda create -n deeplearning pip python=3.5
```

Now that we have created the `deeplearning` virtual environment, we are going to `activate` it so that we can start populating it with Python packages. To do so, open Anaconda's CLI and type the following command:

```
activate deeplearning
```

After typing this command, your CLI prompt should change and include a prefix to indicate that the virtual environment is currently active.

Installing TensorFlow

TensorFlow is a high-level deep learning API written in Python and developed by Google. In this book, TensorFlow will be the backend that supports Keras, our main deep learning API. Follow instructions on the following website: `https://www.tensorflow.org/install/ install_linux#tensorflow_gpu_support`. Choose your OS, and install TensorFlow for Python 3.5 with GPU support.

Installing Keras

Keras is a high-level deep learning API written in Python that supports TensorFlow, CNTK, and Theano as backends. Keras has the main building blocks for building, training, and prototyping deep learning projects. The building blocks in Keras include neural network layers, optimization functions, activation functions, and several tools for working with data and training in general.

Installing `keras` is easy! Inside our `deeplearning` virtual environment, type the following command:

```
pip install keras
```

Installing data visualization and machine learning libraries

In addition to Keras, the main deep learning library used in this book, we are going to install libraries for data visualization and machine learning in general. These libraries provide valuable tools to help developers easily build training pipelines, evaluate and train models more efficiently, and visualize data quickly and effortlessly.

Although there are distributions like Anaconda that provide environments with such libraries already installed by default, we describe the installation procedures here such that the reader learns the process and does not become dependent on pre-packaged third party distributions.

The matplotlib library

The most widely used data visualization library in Python is called `matplotlib`. It enables the quick and easy creation of publication-quality complex plots and graphs, which facilitate understanding data. Matploblib can be installed with `pip` as follows:

```
pip install matplotlib
```

The Jupyter library

Jupyter is another widely used and valuable Python library. It includes Jupyter notebooks, which allow interactive and quick prototyping in Python and other languages on the browser. Jupyter also supports data visualization, including images, video, and audio! Jupyter notebooks can be shared and accessed via a web browser. Jupyter can be installed with `pip` as follows:

```
pip install jupyter
```

The scikit-learn library

Scikit-learn is the leading Python library for machine learning and data science in general. Scikit-learn is open source and built on top of NumPy, SciPy, and matplotlib. It contains a wide range of machine learning models and algorithms, including classification, regression, clustering, dimensionality reduction, model selection, data preprocessing, metrics, and many other valuable things. Scikit-learn can be installed with `pip` as follows:

```
pip install sklearn
```

Now that we have installed our libraries, it is time to make sure everything works as expected.

NVIDIA's CUDA Toolkit and cuDNN

NVIDIA's CUDA Toolkit provides a development environment for creating high-performance GPU-accelerated applications. You can develop, optimize, and deploy your applications on GPU-accelerated embedded systems, workstations, enterprise data centers, cloud-based platforms, and HPC supercomputers using the CUDA Toolkit. The Toolkit includes GPU-accelerated libraries, debugging and optimization tools, a C/C++ compiler, and a runtime library to deploy your application.

 Installing the CUDA Toolkit is easy and can be downloaded from `https://developer.nvidia.com/cuda-downloads`.

NVIDIA's cuDNN is a GPU-accelerated library of primitives for deep neural networks. cuDNN provides highly-tuned implementations for standard routines such as forward and backward convolution, pooling, normalization, and activation layers. cuDNN is part of the NVIDIA Deep Learning SDK.

cuDNN is available for members of the NVIDIA Developer Program. Registration to this program is free and members are given access to the latest NVIDIA SDKs and tools to accelerate building applications in key technology areas such as artificial intelligence, deep learning, accelerated computing, and advanced graphics (`https://developer.nvidia.com/rdp/cudnn-download`).

Now that we have installed NVIDIA's CUDA Toolkit and NVIDIA's cuDNN, our next step is to add environment paths.

The deep learning environment test

We are going to verify our deep learning environment installation by building and training a simple fully-connected neural network to perform classification on images of handwritten digits from the MNIST dataset. MNIST is an introductory dataset that contains 70,000 images, thus enabling us to quickly train a small model on a CPU and extremely fast on the GPU. In this simple example, we are only interested in testing our deep learning setup.

We start by using the `keras` built-in function to download and load the train and test datasets associated with MNIST:

```
import numpy as np
from keras.datasets import mnist
from keras.models import Sequential
from keras.utils import np_utils
from keras.optimizers import SGD
from keras.layers.core import Dense,Activation
```

The training set has 60,000 samples and the test set has 10,000 samples. The dataset is balanced and shuffled, that is, it has a similar number of samples for each class and the orders of the samples are random:

```
(X_train, y_train), (X_test, y_test) = mnist.load_data()
print("Train samples {}, Train labels {}".format(X_train.shape,
y_train.shape))
print("Test samples {}, Test labels {}".format(X_test.shape, y_test.shape))
```

The MNIST dataset contains images of 28 by 28. To train our dense neural network, we need to combine the height and width dimensions of the image to make it unidimensional, while keeping the same batch size, that is, the number of items in the batch. After reshaping the data, we will convert it to floating point and scale it to [-1, 1] following neural networks tricks of the trade described in Yann Lecun's *Efficient Backprop* paper:

```
# reshape to batch size by height * width
h, w = X_train.shape[1:]
X_train = X_train.reshape(X_train.shape[0], h * w)
X_test = X_test.reshape(X_test.shape[0], h * w)
X_train = X_train.astype('float32')
X_test = X_test.astype('float32')
# scale to [0, 1], scale to [0, 2], offset by -1
X_train = (X_train / 255.0) * 2 - 1
X_test = (X_test - 255.0) * 2 - 1
```

For training our network, Keras requires each of our image labels to be in the one-hot representation. In the one-hot representation, we have a vector whose length is equal to the number of classes in which the index that represented the class associated with that label is 1, and 0 otherwise:

```
# convert class vectors to a matrix of one-hot vectors
n_classes = 10
y_train = np_utils.to_categorical(y_train, n_classes)
y_test = np_utils.to_categorical(y_test, n_classes)
```

After having prepared the data, we will define the parameters of our model and instantiate it. We now import from Keras the functions that are necessary to building and training a fully connected neural network. Whereas the `Dense` class instantiates a dense layer, the `Sequential` class allows us to connect these `Dense` layers in a chain. Lastly, we import the Stochastic Gradient Descent optimizer such that we can perform gradient descent on the loss given to the model to update the model parameters. We create a model with two hidden layers. The first layer projects the reshaped h * w image input to `128` nodes, and the second layer projects the `128` nodes down to 10 nodes representing the number of classes in this problem:

```
n_hidden = 128
model = Sequential()
model.add(Dense(n_hidden, activation='tanh', input_dim=h*w))
model.add(Dense(n_classes, activation='softmax'))
model.summary()
```

After defining our model, we define the optimizer's parameters that will be used to update the weights of our model given the loss. We choose a small learning of `0.001` and use the defaults for the other parameters:

```
sgd = SGD(lr=0.001)
```

Finally, we compile the graph of our model setting the `loss` function to `categorical_crossentropy`, which is used in classification problems where each sample belongs to a single class. We use `accuracy` as the reported metric because for this problem we are interested in increasing the `accuracy` metric of our model:

```
model.compile(loss='categorical_crossentropy', optimizer=sgd,
metrics=['accuracy'])
```

We train our model for as many epochs as necessary. One epoch is equivalent to a pass through the entire training data. The batch size is chosen such that it maximizes memory performance by maxing out memory footprint during training. This is very important, especially when using GPUs, such that our models use all the resources available in parallel:

```
model.fit(X_train, y_train, epochs=10, batch_size=128)
```

After training the model, we can check whether our model is generalizing to data that it has not seen by looking at our model's performance on the test data:

```
score = model.evaluate(X_test, y_test, batch_size=128)
print(score)
```

The preceding code block generates the following output:

```
In [9]:  score = model.evaluate(X_test, y_test, batch_size=128)

         10000/10000 [==============================] - 0s 11us/step

In [10]: print(score)

         [0.7495173866271972, 0.7677]
```

Summary

In this chapter, we covered essential knowledge for building and training deep learning models, starting with a simple example based on linear regression. We covered important topics in machine learning such as parameter estimation and backpropagation, loss functions, and diverse neural network layers. We described how to set up a deep learning programming environment that will be used throughout this book. After installing our deep learning programming environment, we trained and evaluated a simple neural network model for the classification of handwritten digits.

In the next chapter, we will cover generative models, explaining the advantages and disadvantages of each class of generative models, including GANs.

Introduction to Generative Models

2

In this chapter, you will learn the basics of generative models. We will start with a brief description of, and comparison between, discriminative and generative models, in which you will learn about the properties of these models. Then, we will focus on a comparison between generative models, and briefly describe how they have been used to achieve state-of-the-art models in fields such as computer vision and audio.

We will also cover other models, and then we will focus on the building blocks of **Generative Adversarial Networks (GANs)**, their strengths, and limitations. This information is valuable because it can inform our decisions when approaching a machine learning problem with GANs, or when learning some new development in GANs.

We will cover the following topics as we progress with this chapter:

- Discriminative and generative models compared
- Generative models
- GANs – building blocks
- GANs – strengths and weaknesses

Discriminative and generative models compared

Broadly speaking, machine learning models can be subdivided into discriminative models and generative models. Discriminative models learn a map from some input to some output. In discriminative models, learning the process that generates the input is not relevant; it will just learn a map from the to the expected output.

Generative models, on the other hand, in addition to learning a map from some input to some output, also learn the process that generates the input and the output.

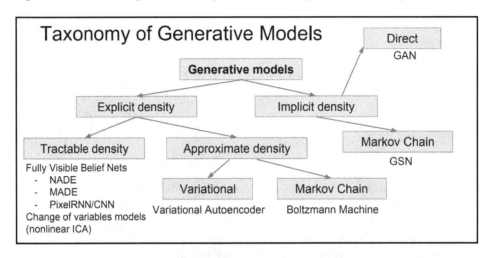

Source: Ian Goodfellow's Tutorial on Generative Adversarial Networks, 2017

In this context, we say that discriminative models estimate $P(y|x)$: the **conditional probability distribution** of y conditioned on x. Note that, in this case, the input x is fixed, known a **priori**, and the discriminative model estimates the probability of y, $P(y|x)$ but does not have any information about the marginal distribution of x nor y independent of the other variables, $P(x)$ and $P(y)$ respectively. Discriminative models can be used to learn a map, $\hat{f}$ that produces outputs that approximates the distribution $P(y|x)$.

Generative models, on the other hand, estimate $P(y, x)$: the **joint probability distribution** of x and y. The joint probability distribution is symmetric and can be written as $P(y|x)p(x)$. Generative models can be used to learn a map, $\hat{f}$ that approximates the distribution $P(y, x)$.

By estimating $P(y, x)$ and knowing that the joint probability is symmetrical, we can use Bayes' theorem to obtain $P(y|x)$ and $P(x|y)$ as we briefly describe below:

$$P(x, y) = P(y, x)$$
$$P(x|y) = \frac{P(x, y)}{P(y)}$$
$$P(y|x) = \frac{P(y, x)}{P(x)} = \frac{P(x, y)}{P(x)}$$

By moving around the terms $P(y)$ and $P(x)$ on the second and third equation we derive Bayes' theorem:

$$P(x|y)P(y) = P(y|x)P(x)$$

Comparing discriminative and generative models

Learning the conditional distribution is easier, because you do not have to make assumptions about the marginal distribution of x or y.

We will use the following diagram to illustrate the differences between discriminative and generative models. We can see two plots with 13 points of a two-dimensional dataset; let's call the blue class labels X_i, and the yellow class labels Y_i:

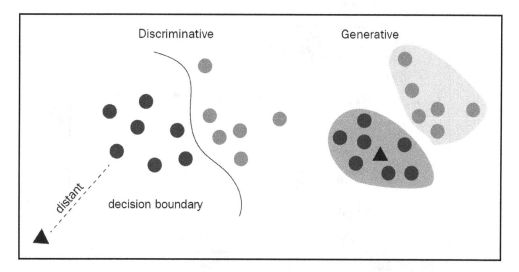

When training a discriminative model, $P(y|x)$, we want to estimate the hidden parameters of the model that describe the conditional probability distribution that provides a decision boundary with an optimal split between the classes at hand. When training a generative model, $P(y, x)$, we want to estimate the parameters that describe the joint probability distribution of x and y.

In addition to predicting the conditional probability, learning the joint probability distribution allows us to sample the learned model to generate new data from x, y, where x is conditioned on y and y is conditioned on x. In the preceding diagram, for example, you could model the joint probability by learning the hidden parameters of a mixture distribution; for example, a Gaussian mixture with one component per class.

Another way to visualize the difference between generative and discriminative models is to look at a graphical depiction of the distribution that is being modeled. In the following diagram, we can see that the depiction of the discriminative model shows a decision boundary that can be used to define the class label, given some fixed data. In this case, predicting $P(y|x)$ can be seen as finding a decision boundary from which the distance of a datapoint to the boundary is proportional to the probability of that datapoint belonging to a class.

In a binary classification task on a single variable-let's call it x-the simplest form of such a model is to find the boundary at which more samples are labeled correctly. In the following figure, the value of x that maximizes the number of correct labels is around 50.

The following depiction of the generative model shows the exact distribution of x in the presence and absence of y. Naturally, given that we know the exact distribution of x and y, we can sample it to generate new data:

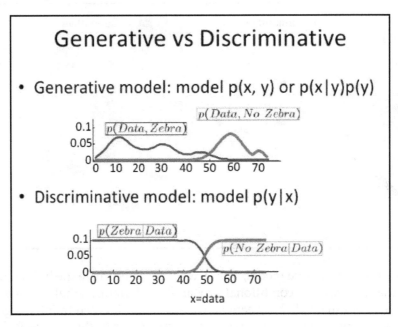

Since generative models handle the hard task of modeling all dependencies and patterns that are in the input and output data, applications of generative models are uncountable. The deep learning field has produced state-of-the-art generative models for applications such as image generation, speech synthesis, and model-based control.

A fascinating aspect of generative models is that they are potentially capable of learning large and complex data distributions with a relatively small number of parameters. Unlike discriminative models, generative models can learn meaningful features from large, unlabeled datasets, a process that requires little to no labeling or human supervision.

Most recent work in generative models has been focused on GANs and likelihood-based methods, including autoregressive models, **Variational Autoencoders** (**VAEs**), and flow-based models. In the following paragraphs, we will describe likelihood-based models and variations thereof. Later, we will describe the GAN framework in detail.

Generative models

We will look into the various approaches of generative models in the following sections.

Autoregressive models

Autoregressive models estimate the conditional distribution of some data y, given some other values of y. For example, in image synthesis, it estimates the conditional distribution of pixels given surrounding or previous pixels; in audio synthesis, it estimates the conditional distribution of audio samples given previous audio samples and spectrograms.

In its simplest linear form, with dependency on the previous time-step only and time-invariant bias term, an autoregressive model can be defined with the following equation:

$$Y_t = \alpha + \sum_{i=1}^{p} \beta_i Y_{t-1} + \epsilon_t,$$

α is a constant term that represents the model's bias, β represents the model's coefficients, Y_{t-1} represents the previous output vector, and ϵ_t is assumed to be white noise. The dependency of the current output on the previous output is explicit in this equation.

Although autoregressive models are sequential in nature, given that the training data is available beforehand, they are normally trained in parallel using the teacher-forcing procedure. In this procedure, the model is not conditioned on its output, but on the real output obtained from the training data.

During inference, the model's output must be used, because we do not have access to the correct output – that is, the model must do autoregression on its own output, hence the name autoregressive model.

Autoregressive models have the advantage of being trained with simple and stable maximum likelihood estimates. This simplicity is counterbalanced by the limited capability of autoregressive models to perform inference in parallel, thus potentially requiring long wait times to generate data.

PixelCNN is one of the most famous autoregressive models for image synthesis. You can refer to the following paper for more details: https://www.semanticscholar.org/paper/ Conditional-Image-Generation-with-PixelCNN-Decoders-Oord-Kalchbrenner/ 8e4ab54564fb492dcae9a1e862aedd3e52fb258b.

In the following figure, we show an image of faces generated with PixelCNN:

Source: Conditional Image Generation with PixelCNN Decoders (https://arxiv.org/abs/1606.05328)

WaveNet is one of the most famous autoregressive generative models for audio-synthesis. You can refer to the following paper for more details about WaveNet, available at: `https://arxiv.org/pdf/1609.03499.pdf`. The following diagram describes WaveNet's graph:

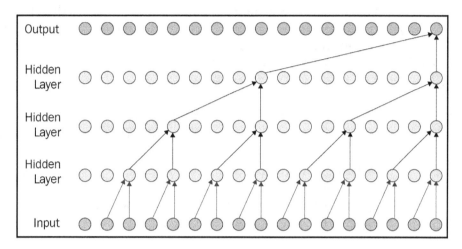

Source: WaveNet: A Generative Model for Raw Audio (`https://arxiv.org/abs/1609.03499`)

Variational autoencoders

Auto-encoder models are used to model $p(x, z)$, the joint probability of x, the observed data, and z, the latent variable. The joint probability $p(x, z)$ is normally factorized as $p(x|z)p(z)$. During inference, we are interested in finding good values of z to produce observed data – that is, we are interested in learning $p(z|x)$, the posterior probability of z given x. Using Bayes' rule, we can rewrite the posterior as follows:

$$\frac{p(x|z)p(z)}{p(x)}.$$

Close inspection of this equation reveals that computing the evidence, the marginal distribution of the data $p(x)$, is hardly possible and normally intractable. We first try to circumvent this barrier by computing an approximation of the evidence. We do it by using variational inference, and, instead, estimating the parameters of a known distribution $q(z)$ that is the least divergent from the posterior $p(z \mid x)$. Variational inference approximates the posterior $p(z \mid x)$ with a family of distributions $q_\lambda(z|x)$, where the variational λ parameter indexes the family of distributions. This can be done by minimizing the KL divergence between $q(z)$ and $p(z|x)$, as described in the following equation:

$$D_{KL}\left(q(z) \parallel p(z|x)\right) = \mathbb{E}[\log\ q(z)] - \mathbb{E}[\log\ p(z \mid x)]$$
$$= \mathbb{E}[\log\ q(z)] - \mathbb{E}[\log\ p(x, z)] + \log\ p(x)$$

Unfortunately, using $q(z)$ does not circumvent the problem, and we are still faced with computing the evidence $p(x)$. At this point, we give up on computing the exact evidence and focus on estimating an **Evidence Lower Bound (ELBO)**. The ELBO sets the perfect scenario for Variational Autoencoders, and is computed by removing $p(x)$ of the previous equation and inverting the signs, giving:

$$ELBO = \mathbb{E}[\log\ p(x, z)] - \mathbb{E}[\log\ q(z)]]$$

VAEs consist of an encoder Q parametrized by θ, and a decoder P parametrized by ϕ. The encoder is trained to maximize the posterior probability of a z latent vector, given the x, $Q_\theta(z|x)$. data. The decoder is trained to maximize the probability of the data x given the latent representation z latent vector, $P\phi(x|z)$. Informally speaking, the encoder learns to compress the data into a latent representation, and the decoder learns to decompress the data from the latent representation. The VAE loss is defined as follows:

$$L_{VAE}(\theta, \phi) = -\mathbb{E}_{z \sim q_\theta(z|x_i)}[\log\ p_\phi(x_i \mid z)] + D_{KL}(q_\theta(z|x_i) \parallel p(z))$$

The first term represents the reconstruction loss, or the expectation of the negative probability. The second term is a regularize term that was derived in our problem setup.

Unlike autoregressive models, VAEs are normally easy to run in parallel during training and inference. Conversely, they are normally harder to optimize than autoregressive models.

Deep feature-consistent VAE is one of the best models for image generation using VAEs. The following figure shows the faces generated by the model. From a qualitative perspective, image samples produced with VAEs tend to be blurry.

Source: Deep feature-consistent VAE (https://arxiv.org/abs/1610.00291)

Reversible flows

Reversible flow models have been gaining attention in the research community, given their impressive results in image and speech synthesis. Flow-based generative models are reversible in nature, and a single model P with a parameter θ estimates both the conditional probability of the data x given the latent vector z, $P_\theta(x|z)$, and the probability of the z latent vector given the x data, $P_\theta(z|x)$. This characteristic of reversible flow models enables exact latent-variable inference and log-likelihood evaluation without any approximation, thus representing an advantage over VAEs.

Reversible flow models are comprised of multiple layers of flow. Each flow layer uses a neural network that is not reversible to compute the parameters of an affine coupling layer that scales and translates the data. Since scaling and translation are reversible operations, each flow layer is a bijection assuring the following:

$$x = f_0 \circ f1 \circ \cdots f_k(z)$$
$$z = f_k^{-1} \circ f_{k-1}^{-1} \circ \cdots f_0^{-1}(x)$$

This brings with it another very nice property: by restricting each flow layer to be bijective, the likelihood can be calculated directly by using the change of variables. Without loss of generality, let's assume the latent variable z is a spherical Gaussian, and describe the maximum likelihood in the context of a reversible flow model:

$$z \sim N(z; 0, \boldsymbol{I})$$

$$\log \ p_\theta(x) = \log \ p_\theta(z) + \sum_{i=1}^{k} \log | \det(\boldsymbol{J}(\boldsymbol{f}_i^{-1}(x))) |.$$

The first term is the log-likelihood of a spherical Gaussian, and it penalizes the l_2 norm. The second term arises from the change of variables, and $\boldsymbol{J}$ is the Jacobian. The log-determinant of the Jacobian rewards any layer for increasing the volume of the space during the forward pass.

A closer look to the preceding equation shows that, unlike VAEs, by being bijective, reversible flow models allow for the direct computation of the evidence $p_\theta(x)$, which should be closer to the true evidence than computing an ELBO.

Similar to VAEs, reversible flow models provide efficient training and inference in parallel. In addition, and similar to VAEs, flow-based models allow for manipulations of the latent space, including interpolations between data points or conditional synthesis based on latent space clustering.

Glow is one of the best models for image generation using flow-based models. The following figure shows the faces generated by the model. We invite the reader to compare this sample to the other samples provided in this chapter:

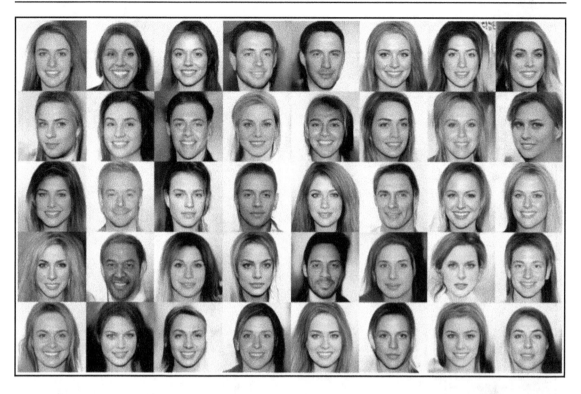

Source: Glow: Generative Flow with Invertible 1x1 Convolutions (https://arxiv.org/abs/1807.03039)

Researchers at NVIDIA have applied flow-based generative models to speech synthesis. Refer to the paper in the following link for further reference:
https://arxiv.org/abs/1811.00002

Generative adversarial networks

GANs are evolving rather quickly, and are receiving a considerable amount of attention from the research community. Yann LeCun's comment, expressing that the GAN framework is the most interesting idea in the last 10 years of machine learning, shows evidence of the perceived importance of the framework.

The following is a figure representing applications of the GAN framework:

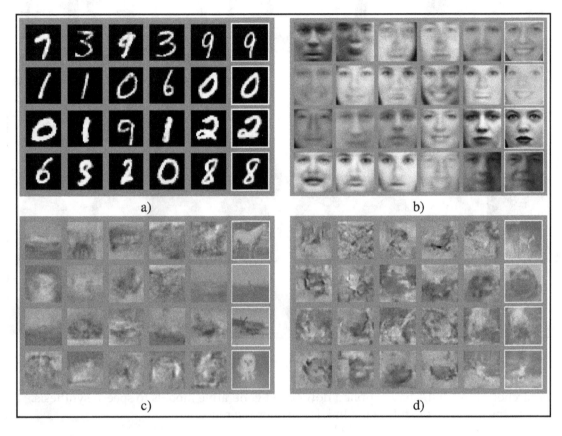

Source: Generative Adversarial Nets (https://arxiv.org/abs/1406.2661)

The GAN framework has been widely used to generate data from many domains. Examples of data generation with GANs include text-to-image synthesis, image super-resolution, and symbolic music generation. In addition to data generation, the GAN framework has also been used for unsupervised feature learning.

GANs were first described in the landmark paper *Generative Adversarial Nets* by Ian Goodfellow published in 2014. The setup of the framework uses an adversarial process to estimate the parameters of two models by iteratively and concomitantly training a discriminator network D and a generator net G.

One of the main advantages of GANs is that, unlike other approaches that use approximation methods to compute intractable functions or inference, such as VAE, GANs do not require an approximation method.

Informally speaking, the discriminator network plays the role of an investigator that learns to distinguish between samples that are real (samples that come from the distribution that generates the real data), and samples that are fake (samples produced by the generator). The generator network plays the role of a counterfeiter that uses feedback from the discriminator to learn how to produce samples that are capable of fooling the discriminator. This informal description already calls attention to the following potential issues with the GAN framework:

- A weak investigator might be easily fooled by the generator.
- An investigator without enough capacity might not learn to distinguish the data properly.
- An investigator that disregards variety can be fooled with a single example.

GANs have been successfully applied to many domains. In computer vision, noticeable applications of GAN include progressive growing of GANs and pix2pixHD, which we will learn to implement in this book. The following diagram illustrates our description of the GAN framework, and is the simplest base of a GAN implementation:

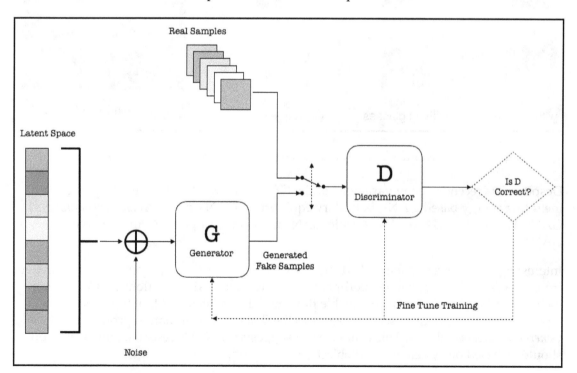

The early paper *Unsupervised Representation Learning with Deep Convolutional Generative Adversarial Networks* by *Alec Radford et al.* has many exciting applications of GANs. In addition to using a trained discriminator for image classification tasks that shows competitive performance with other unsupervised algorithms, they show that the generator has interesting vector arithmetic properties that allows for manipulation of semantic qualities. The following figure from Alec Radford's paper shows an application of GAN vector arithmetic:

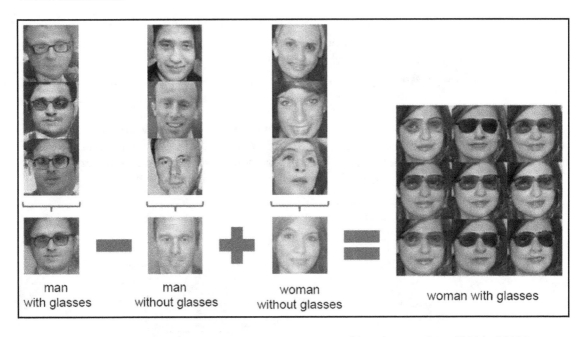

man with glasses   man without glasses   woman without glasses   woman with glasses

Source: Unsupervised Representation Learning with Deep Convolutional GANs (https://arxiv.org/abs/1511.06434)

Despite of its recency, many variations of the GAN framework have been proposed, including energy-based GANs, boundary equilibrium GANs, mix-GANs, least-squares GANs, Wasserstein GANs, Wasserstein GANs with gradient penalty, and relativistic GANs.

Interestingly, in a recent paper called *Are GANs created equal? A large-scale study*, researchers from Google Brain performed experiments with multiple GAN variations and VAEs, not including relativistic GANs or reversible flow models, and claimed that there was no evidence that the variations were superior to the first GAN formulation proposed in *Generative Adversarial Nets*. This claim clearly suggests that GAN research and evaluation should be based on systematic and objective evaluation.

Progressive growing of GANs has been state-of-the-art in image generation using GANs. Progressive growing of GANs allows the generation of 1,024 by 1,024 high-resolution images. In the following figure, we provide a selection of celebrity faces generated with progressive growing of GANs:

Source: Progressive Growing of GANs (https://arxiv.org/abs/1710.10196)

Another impressive development in GANs is pix2pixHD. This is a method for high-resolution (for example, 2048 x 1024) photorealistic image-to-image translation. The method has been used to synthesize portraits from face label maps and turning semantic label maps into photo realistic images. The following is an example of an input label:

Source: pix2pixHD project page (https://tcwang0509.github.io/pix2pixHD/)

The following is the corresponding synthesized figure:

Source: pix2pixHD project page (https://tcwang0509.github.io/pix2pixHD/)

GANs – building blocks

A GAN is informally described as an iterative game played between a detective and a counterfeiter; while the detective's goal is to minimize its loss by learning to identify real data as real and fake data as fake, the counterfeiter's goal is to minimize its loss by learning to fool the detective by transforming random noise into fake data. This informal definition can be described using the following figure:

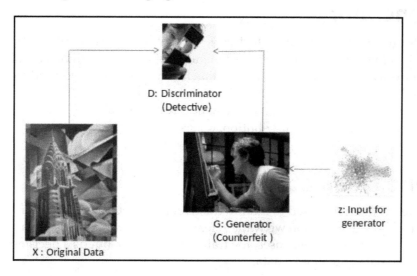

Source: Generative Adversarial Networks – A Deep Learning Architecture (https://hackernoon.com/generative-adversarial-networks-a-deep-learning-architecture-4253b6d12347)

Let's enumerate the building blocks of GANs and define the GAN framework formally:

- The discriminator, D, a detective
- The generator, G, a counterfeiter
- Real data, x, (images, audio, text)
- Fake data, $G(z)$, (images, audio, text)
- Random noise, z, (uniform, Gaussian)
- The discriminator's loss, $V(D)$
- The generator's loss, $V(G)$

The discriminator

In the original GAN framework, the discriminator (detective) D is a function $f : x \mapsto y$, where x is some input sample in $\mathbb{R}^d$, and y is a scalar. When using GANs to produce images, for example, in some formulation x represents an image and $y = D(x)$ represents D's predicted probability that x comes from the real distribution.

The generator

The generator (counterfeiter) G is a function $f : z \mapsto \tilde{x}$, where z is a noise vector in $\mathbb{R}^m$ and $G(z) = \tilde{x} \in \mathbb{R}^d$ is some data produced by the generator. Note that the dimensionality of the noise vector does not necessarily match the dimensionality of the data produced by the generator. When using GANs to produce images, for example, $G(z) = \tilde{x}$ represents an image. We use ~ to differentiate between data that comes from the real distribution x, and data that comes from the generators distribution, $\tilde{x}$.

Real and fake data

Real and fake are the terms used to refer to the data used in GANs. Real refers to the data that comes from the distribution we want to learn, and fake refers to the data produced by the generator. In most GAN use cases, the training procedure builds a decision boundary between all real data and all fake data.

In cases where there is not enough data, triplet loss learning can be used so that the discriminator also learns to differentiate between the target real data and non-target real data. This approach has been used in the paper *Attacking Speaker Recognition with Deep Generative Models*.

Random noise

Interestingly, the generator itself does not have any source of randomness because it is not a parametric model. The generator is a non-parametric model with fixed coefficients; that is, the coefficients are not sampled from a parametric distribution.

The generator's source of randomness comes from the random noise z vector and the generator itself represents a map from this noise vector to some data. The random noise z vector is sampled from a known distribution, such as the uniform distribution or the Gaussian distribution.

Discriminator and generator loss

Given the setup that we have described, D and G play a iterative two-player minimax game with the value function $V(G, D)$:

$$\min_{G} \max_{D} V(D, G) = \mathbb{E}_{x \sim p_{data}}[log D(x)] + \mathbb{E}_{z \sim p_z}[log(1 - D(G(z)))]$$

Literally speaking, it minimizes its loss when D(x) is equal to 1 and D(G(z)) is equal to 0, that is, when the discriminator's probability of real is 1 for real data and 0 for fake data. Hence, the discriminator is maximizing the outputs from D(X) and D(G(z)).

The generator, on the other hand, minimizes its loss when D(G(z)) is equal to 1, that is, when the discriminator's probability of real data as fake data is 1. Hence, the generator is minimizing the outputs from D(G(z)).

The objective function described in the preceding equation is equivalent to minimizing the **Jensen-Shannon** (**JS**) divergence between the distributions, as described in the paper *Generative Adversarial Nets* by *Ian Goodfellow et al.* The JS divergence is a symmetric and smoothed version of the **Kullback-Leibler** (**KL**) divergence, described in the paper *On information and sufficiency* by *Kullback and Leibler*. Note that in the following equation, D stands for divergence, not discriminator:

$$D_{JS}(P \| Q) = \frac{1}{2} D_{KL}(P \| M) + \frac{1}{2} D_{KL}(Q \| M),$$

D_{KL} on a continuous support is defined as follows:

$$D_{KL}(P \| Q) = \int_{-\infty}^{+\infty} p(x) \log \frac{q(x)}{p(x)} dx$$

A closer look at the KL divergence described earlier shows a few problems with respect to exploding losses when the support of P is not contained in Q. In the next section, we will address this topic within the context of the strengths and weaknesses of GANs.

GANs – strengths and weaknesses

GANs are one of the hottest topics in deep learning nowadays! The GAN framework has many strengths compared to other frameworks that we will enumerate in this section. Naturally, GANs also have weaknesses and challenges that we will describe.

One of the advantages of GANs is the use of the discriminator as an embedding space that does not require any label. This has been described in the paper *Feature learning by inpainting* by *Deepak Pathak et al.* and *Unsupervised representation learning with deep convolutional generative adversarial networks* by *Alec Radford et al.* In these papers, the authors have used GANs to learn features in an unsupervised fashion. Another amazing strength of the GAN framework is that it circumvents the potentially difficult challenge of designing an objective function for the task at hand.

There are also many weaknesses in GANs related to training and evaluating them. For example, unlike optimization problems, whose cost function relies on maximizing the likelihood of the data given the model's parameters, GANs rely on a minimax game between the discriminator and the generator.

It can be seen from the previous equation that KL-based objective functions suffer from exploding loss when the support of the real P distribution is not contained on the other Q distribution. In other words, the KL divergence goes to infinity if there is some x, such that $Q(x) = 0$ where $P(x) > 0$.

Regarding the GAN loss and others, the *Wasserstein GAN* paper provides a thorough comparison of different distances, and explains that there are distributions where JS, KL, and even total variation divergence do not converge and have gradients always equal to 0.

Another problem with the original GAN objective function in the KL divergence equation is that the sigmoid function saturates quickly and, for this reason, will barely consider the distance of a sample to the decision boundary formed with the sigmoid. In the *Least Squares Generative Adversarial Networks* paper, Xudong Mao et al. claim that the original GAN loss will produce vanishing gradients when updating the generator with fake samples that are on the correct side, but still far from real data.

Furthermore, although an equilibrium is reached when the discriminator outputs 0.5 for the probability of fake data, the game is not over for the discriminator, as it can continue to increase the probability of real data, possibly bringing complications to the training process. We will briefly address this issue later in the book and describe, among other things, a solution proposed in The *Relativistic Discriminator: a key element missing from standard GAN* paper proposed by *Alexia Jolicoeur-Martineau*.

Going further, in GANs, you train two models, a discriminator and a generator, under the assumption that the models have enough capacity to model the data, and that the capacity of the models is comparable; that is, one model cannot overpower the other. This condition is handled by creating models that have approximately the same number of parameters.

In addition, during training the models perform parameter updates alternately, and this requires choosing learning rates so that neither model overpowers the other, for example, by taking too large of a step. This is a known problem in GANs, and is normally circumvented by carefully choosing the learning rate.

Finally, one of the most important assumptions, described in the seminal GAN paper, is that the model will converge to the true distribution if the discriminator and generator have infinite capacity and there is a large amount of data. These assumptions are rather strong, and work done by Sanjeev Aurora et al. in their papers *Generalization and equilibrium in generative adversarial nets* and *Do GANs actually learn the distribution? An empirical study* has investigated this assumption and evaluated GAN networks using the birthday paradox.

Furthermore, work in the paper *A note on the evaluation of generative models* sheds theoretical and empirical light on this assumption: they describe that there is considerable independence between sample quality and likelihood, showing that high likelihood and sample quality do not necessarily imply a good model, given independence between pixels. In natural images, neighboring pixels are normally not independent.

Despite of all these challenges, researchers continue training GANs and producing mind-blowing results.

Summary

We started this chapter by describing and comparing discriminative and generative models. We introduced a few probabilistic concepts, including Bayes' theorem, and described mathematically and visually the probabilistic models learned by discriminative and generative models. Next, we provided information about multiple types of generative models, including GANs, Variational Autoencoders, and reversible flow models. We mathematically derived these models, compared them to each other, showed examples of their usage, and enumerated their advantages and disadvantages.

In addition, we described the building blocks of GANs, enumerating the individual components used in the framework and examining how they can be used. Finally, we briefly exposed their strengths and limitations.

In the next chapter, you will learn how to implement your first GAN.

Section 2: Training GANs 2

In this section, you will learn how to train simple GAN models, come to understand the challenges involved in training GANs, learn to evaluate GAN samples, and lastly, learn how to improve GANs with different architectures and loss functions.

The following chapters will be covered in this section:

- Chapter 3, *Implementing Your First GAN*
- Chapter 4, *Evaluating Your First GAN*
- Chapter 5, *Improving Your First GAN*

Implementing Your First GAN

3

In this chapter, you will learn the basics about implementing and training **Generative Adversarial Network (GAN)** models for image synthesis. You will learn to implement a Generator and Discriminator a GAN. You will then learn to implement your loss function and use it to train your GAN framework. You will also learn to visualize the samples from your first GAN. We will focus on the well-known CIFAR-10 dataset with 60,000 32 by 32 colour images in 10 classes.

The following topics will be covered in this chapter:

- Imports
- Implementing the Generator and the Discriminator
- Auxiliary functions
- Training your GAN

Technical requirements

In this chapter we will focus on the CIFAR10 that is included with Keras.

We will rely on the software libraries included in our Docker container available at `https://github.com/rafaelvalle/hands_on_gans_with_keras/blob/master/Dockerfile`

You can visit the GitHub repo of this book for the full code files from the following link: `https://github.com/PacktPublishing/Hands-On-Generative-Adversarial-Networks-with-Keras`.

Imports

In this section, we provide a list of libraries and methods that will be used in our first GAN implementation. The following code block is the list of libraries to be used:

```
import matplotlib
matplotlib.use("Agg")
import matplotlib.pylab as plt
from math import ceil
import numpy as np
from keras.models import Sequential, Model
from keras.layers import Input, ReLU, LeakyReLU, Dense
from keras.layers.core import Activation, Reshape
from keras.layers.normalization import BatchNormalization
from keras.layers.convolutional import Conv2D, Conv2DTranspose
from keras.layers.core import Flatten
from keras.optimizers import SGD, Adam
from keras.datasets import cifar10
from keras import initializers
```

Lines one through four `import` libraries and methods that are necessary for plotting.

Line five imports `numpy`, which is used for overall data operations, including generation, manipulation, and arithmetic.

Lines 6 through 13 `import` the necessary methods for building our Generator and Discriminator models and implementing our training routine. Although the names are self-descriptive, we will describe the methods when they are used.

Line 14 is a `keras` routine that gives quick access to the data, including downloading it if it's not available on your computer.

Implementing a Generator and Discriminator

In this section, we will learn how to implement a Generator and Discriminator that is commonly used in the GAN framework. Within the possible network architectures, our research community has focused on network architectures similar to DCGAN and Resnet. The DCGAN architecture was first described in the paper *Unsupervised Representation Learning with Deep Convolutional* by *A. Radford et al*. Resnet-like GAN architectures were probably first used in the *Wasserstein GAN* paper by *Martin Arjovsky et al* and first described in *Deep Residual Learning for Image Recognition* by *K. He et al*.

At the time Resnets were proposed, Resnets and their residual connections were essential for achieving state-of-the-art results in computer vision tasks. The concept of residual connections extended to other architectures and domains, and has been extensively used by the deep learning community. The following figure illustrates a residual connection between the input x and it's output on the function F, producing $F(x) + x$:

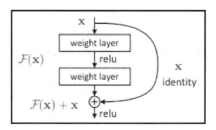

Illustration of the residual connection. Source: Deep Residual Learning for Image Recognition (https://arxiv.org/abs/1512.03385)

The architectures used for Generators and Discriminators in GANs are largely based on convolutional architectures, with transposed convolutions in the Generator and regular convolutions in the Discriminator. There has been research in recurrent GAN architectures that use RNNs and LSTMs. The contribution of recurrent GAN models, however, remains marginal compared to the results obtained using convolutional or fully convolutional architectures.

When designing the Generator and the Discriminator, it is important that their architectures have comparable capacity. This characteristic is important given that the original GAN framework describes a zero-sum non-cooperative game and a Nash equilibrium (https://en.wikipedia.org/wiki/Nash_equilibrium) might not be reached if one network has more capacity than the other. In this context, most of the Generator and Discriminator design is symmetrical. In the following diagram of the DCGAN architecture, we can see that the architecture looks like the other in reverse:

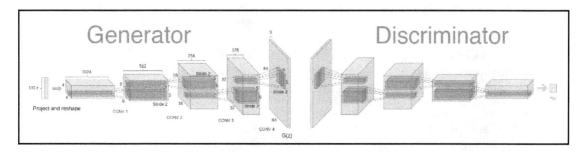

Source: Gluom's mxnet repo (https://gluon.mxnet.io/chapter14_generative-adversarial-networks/dcgan.html)

In the preceding diagram, the Generator learns a map from a vector z to an image. The Discriminator maps the image to a single probability value, indicating that in this GAN framework the Discriminator directly computes the probability that a sample is real or fake.

Generator

The Generator architecture is a map from a low-dimensional space to a higher dimensional space G(z), wherein, fake images produced by the generator live. In other words, the generator samples z and projects it into some multidimensional, for example $\mathbf{R}^{16}$ if the images produced by the Generator are 4 by 4. In fully convolutional Generator architectures, transposed convolutions are used in the Generator to increase the data-dimensionality. Our first Generator implementation will be based on DCGAN, a non-fully convolutional architecture. Let's start by analyzing the following diagram:

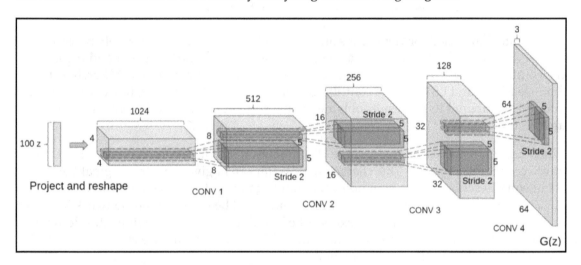

Generator DCGAN architecture. Source: Unsupervised Representation Learning with Deep Convolutional Generative Adversarial Networks (https://arxiv.org/abs/1511.06434).

The DCGAN's Generator diagram shows an unconditional architecture: that is, the Generator produces images using the z vector only, and is not conditioned on extra inputs such as class labels. Let's take a look at the first few lines of the implementation:

```
def build_cifar10_generator(ngf=64, z_dim=128):
    """ Builds CIFAR10 DCGAN Generator Model
    PARAMS
    ------
    ngf: number of generator filters
    z_dim: number of dimensions in latent vector
```

```
RETURN
------
G: keras sequential
"""
init = initializers.RandomNormal(stddev=0.02)
G = Sequential()
# Dense 1: 2x2x512
G.add(Dense(2*2*ngf*8, input_shape=(z_dim, ),
        use_bias=True, kernel_initializer=init))
G.add(Reshape((2, 2, ngf*8)))
G.add(BatchNormalization())
G.add(LeakyReLU(0.2))
```

We start by implementing the function header and defining its inputs. In our implementation, the Generator takes the initial number of Generator filters, ngf, and the dimensionality of the z latent vector as input. During the training implementation, we will describe how z is being sampled.

We use the RandomNormal method to instantiate a weight initializer that samples a normal distribution with mean 0 and 0.02 standard deviation.

We instantiate the Sequential class onto which we are going to add our neural network blocks, including layers, weight normalizations, and non-linearities.

As the DCGAN's Generator image portrays, we add a `Dense` layer that projects the latent vector z to a vector of size 2*2*ngf*8. This operation projects z to a larger number of dimensions so that, after reshaping, we can apply transposed convolutions and gradually increase the dimension of each layer output until it reaches the dimension of our target data.

GANs are known to be sensitive to parameter initialization. We use the init variable to initialize the weights of the Dense layer with a Gaussian distribution with mean 0 and 0.02 standard deviation. These parameters have worked well in this model setup and in other GAN implementations. In line 87, we reshape this tensor to have the shape 2, 2, ngf * 8. This can be interpreted as a 2 by 2 tensor with ngf * 8 channels

Following DCGAN's Generator architecture, we include `BatchNormalization` and the `LeakyReLU` non-linearity with the alpha parameter set to 0.2.

`BatchNormalization` applies an affine transformation to an input normalized to have 0 mean and 1 standard deviation. It is believed that inputs normalized to these parameters can help with the flow of gradients between layers of the networks. `BatchNormalization` consists of two operations.

First, `BatchNormalization` normalizes the input, x_i, with batch statistics μ_b and σ_b^2:

$$\hat{x}_i = \frac{x_i - \mu_b}{\sqrt{\sigma_b^2 + \epsilon}}$$

Next, `BatchNormalization` applies an affine transformation to the normalized input $\hat{x}_i$:

$$y_i = \gamma\hat{x}_i + \beta$$

Note that `BatchNormalization` is sensitive to batch size because it computes statistics based on the current batch. We know from statistics that the mean and the standard deviation are statistics that are sensitive to the size of the data – the smaller the batch size, the noisier the estimates of the mean and standard deviation are going to be. Interestingly, this noisier estimate can have a positive regularization effect on the network.

For batch sizes equal to a single input size, an exponential average is used to compute the mean and standard deviation. The `BatchNormalization` layer in Keras has one very important parameter, called `axis`, which defines the axis that should be batch-normalized.

The `LeakyRelu` non-linearity, as the name implies, is a leaky version of the ReLU non-linearity that allows for some gradient, although small, for values equal or less than zero. The alpha argument controls the slope of the `LeakyReLU` non-linearity:

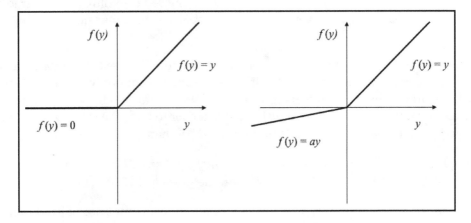

Following the DCGAN architecture, we now must add blocks of transposed convolutions to the Generator, followed by `BatchNormalization` and `LeakyReLU`, as shown in the following code snippet:

```
# Conv 1: 4x4x256
G.add(Conv2DTranspose(ngf*4, kernel_size=5, strides=2,
        padding='same',use_bias=True,
        kernel_initializer=init))
G.add(BatchNormalization())
G.add(LeakyReLU(0.2))
```

Keras provides a single method for performing 2D transposed convolutions, called `Conv2DTranspose`. This is the method we use in this code-block. We are going to add four of these layers, and on each one of the layers we are going to decrease the number of channels by half (ngf * [8, 4, 2, 1]). At the same time, the 2d transposed convolutions with `strides=2` will increase the height and width by twice as much as before, from 4 by 4 to 8 by 8.

We can achieve a similar effect as the 2D transposed convolution with stride 2 by first upsampling the data, and then calling a regular 2D convolution with `border_mode='same'` as follows:

```
G.add(UpSampling2D(size=(2, 2)))
G.add(Convolution2D(ngf*4, 5, 5, border_mode='same'))
```

The UpSampling layers in Keras resize the input by repeating or interpolating the non-channel dimensions of the data by the values provided in the `size` argument. In this example, we're using the `UpSampling2D` layer to resize the row and column dimensions by two. In Keras, this can be done with the TensorFlow's backend, which supports nearest neighbor and bilinear interpolation.

 Computerphile has a great video on nearest neighbor and bilinear interpolation: `https://www.youtube.com/watch?v=AqscP7rc8_M`.

Let's take a look at the effect of each interpolation technique in the following figure. We can see that with nearest interpolation, upsampling simply copies existing pixel values. With bilinear interpolation, on the other hand, the target values are an interpolation between existing values, hence producing a blurry result.

Let's visit these interpolation methods briefly:

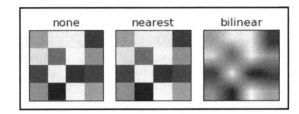

None, nearest and bilinear interpolation. Source: Matplotlib (https://matplotlib.org/1.5.3/examples/images_
contours_and_fields/interpolation_methods.html)

Now that we have briefly described the upsampling layer and upsampling techniques, let's describe the convolution layer, especially the Convolution2D layer. The convolution layers in Keras provide an easy interface to add filters to our models whose coefficients will be updated during training. The interface with the method is simple, and the main parameters of the Convolution2D layer are as follows:

- `nb_filter`: The number of convolution filters.
- `nb_row, nb_col`: The number of rows and columns in the convolution kernel.
- `init`: The name of the initialization function for weights of the layer. This function exists in many layers in Keras.
- `activation`: The name of the activation function to be used. It is used as a replacement for inserting an activation function layer.
- `border_mode`: Support valid, same, or full. It is known as padding in other deep learning frameworks. Valid restricts the kernel to traversing only within the image; same pads the image so that the output has the same size as the image; full pads the image so that every pixel will be visited as many times as the size of the filter.

The 2D transposed convolution layer that we just used transforms and upscales the input. We are going to use two more of these blocks in the following code snippet:

```
# Conv 2: 8x8x128
G.add(Conv2DTranspose(ngf*2, kernel_size=5, strides=2, padding='same',
                      use_bias=True, kernel_initializer=init))
G.add(BatchNormalization())
G.add(LeakyReLU(0.2))

# Conv 3: 16x16x64
G.add(Conv2DTranspose(ngf, kernel_size=5, strides=2, padding='same',
                      use_bias=True, kernel_initializer=init))
```

```
G.add(BatchNormalization())
G.add(LeakyReLU(0.2))
```

Finally, we add a 2D transposed convolution layer to project the last output of our Generator to 3 channels so that it matches the number of color channels in our image data. This layer has a `tanh` activation to map the range of our Generator to the range of the image data that we linearly scaled from [0, 255] to [-1, 1]. We wrap it up by showing the model summary by invoking the `summary` function and returning the Generator:

```
# Conv 4: 32x32x3
G.add(Conv2DTranspose(3, kernel_size=5, strides=2, padding='same',
                      use_bias=True, kernel_initializer=init))
G.add(Activation('tanh'))
print("\nGenerator")
G.summary()

return G
```

Discriminator

The Discriminator architecture is a map from a multidimensional space where images live to a much smaller dimensional space: the number line. This number line will be used to compute the probability that the input image is fake or real. Following the trend in computer vision, the Discriminator architecture uses convolution layers to learn this projection. Our first Discriminator implementation is based on a fully convolutional architecture called DCGAN. We provide DCGAN's discriminator diagram below.

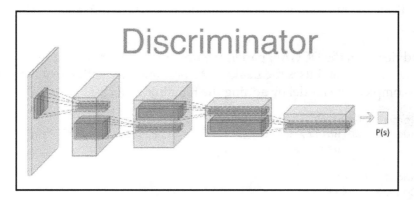

Discriminator DCGAN architectures. Source: Gluom's mxnet repo (https://gluon.mxnet.io/chapter14_generative-adversarial-networks/dcgan.html)

The DCGAN's Discriminator diagram shows an architecture with four convolution layers. Let's look at our function header:

```
def build_cifar10_discriminator(ndf=64, image_shape=(32, 32, 3)):
    """ Builds CIFAR10 DCGAN Discriminator Model
    PARAMS
    ------
    ndf: number of discriminator filters
    image_shape: 32x32x3
    RETURN
    ------
    D: keras sequential
    """
    init = initializers.RandomNormal(stddev=0.02)
    D = Sequential()
```

The function header defines two inputs that take the number of Discriminator filters, ndf, and the shape of the input image. Like in our Generator implementation, we start by instantiating a `Sequential()` object, onto which we will add the network layers and other parts of the network. Let's take a look at the first layer that will be added:

```
    # Conv 1: 16x16x64
    D.add(Conv2D(ndf, kernel_size=5, strides=2, padding='same',
 use_bias=True,
                 kernel_initializer=init, input_shape=image_shape))
    D.add(LeakyReLU(0.2))
```

The DCGAN Discriminator consists of blocks with one 2D Convolution each. The first block has a 2D convolution with `ndf` channels. On each subsequent 2D convolution, we are going to duplicate the number of channels and decrease the width and height by half by using stride `2`.

Following advice from the DCGAN paper, the first block does not include `BatchNormalization` and uses the `LeakyReLU` non-linearity with the alpha parameter set to `0.2`. We complete the model by adding the remaining blocks:

```
    # Conv 2: 8x8x128
    D.add(Conv2D(ndf*2, kernel_size=5, strides=2, padding='same',
                 use_bias=True, kernel_initializer=init))
    D.add(BatchNormalization())
    D.add(LeakyReLU(0.2))
    # Conv 3: 4x4x256
    D.add(Conv2D(ndf*4, kernel_size=5, strides=2, padding='same',
                 use_bias=True, kernel_initializer=init))
    D.add(BatchNormalization())
    D.add(LeakyReLU(0.2))
    # Conv 4: 2x2x512
```

```
D.add(Conv2D(ndf*8, kernel_size=5, strides=2, padding='same',
             use_bias=True, kernel_initializer=init))
D.add(BatchNormalization())
D.add(LeakyReLU(0.2))
```

Finally, we complete the model architecture by flattening the output of the last convolution layer so that we can apply a `dense` layer to it. The `dense` layer projects the input to a single number that is wrapped between 0 and 1 by using the `sigmoid` non-linearity, as shown in the following code snippet. We interpret this number as the probability that the data is real:

```
# Flatten: 2x2x512 -> (2048)
D.add(Flatten())

# Dense Layer
D.add(Dense(1, kernel_initializer=init))
D.add(Activation('sigmoid'))

print("\nDiscriminator")
D.summary()

return D
```

Now that we have defined both models, let's define a few auxiliary functions that will be used to train our GAN models.

Auxiliary functions

We are going to use three auxiliary functions to get the data, plot the images, and plot the losses.

The function to get the data uses the Keras `cifar10` class, converts it to fp32, 32-bit floating point, and scales it to [-1, 1]. Scaling images to [-1, 1] is a common practice when training GANs on image data that bounds the range of the output, possibly avoiding explosions:

```
def get_data():
    # load cifar10 data
    (X_train, y_train), (X_test, y_test) = cifar10.load_data()
    # convert train and test data to float32
    X_train = X_train.astype(np.float32)
    X_test = X_test.astype(np.float32)
    # scale train and test data to [-1, 1]
    X_train = (X_train / 255) * 2 - 1
    X_test = (X_train / 255) * 2 - 1

    return X_train, X_test
```

The method below is used to plot a grid with images. It takes a tensor with the images and the full path where the image will be saved as input. Unlike other optimization problems, where analysis of the empirical risk is a strong indicator of progress, in GANs the decrease in loss is not always correlated with an increase in image quality, and so, authors still rely on a visual inspection of generated images.

Based on visual inspections, some researchers confirm that they have not observed mode collapse, or that their framework is robust to mode collapse if some criteria is met. This is addressed in papers such as *Wasserstein GAN, Improved Training of Wasserstein GAN*, and the *Least Squares Generative Adversarial Networks*. In practice, GitHub issues where practitioners report mode collapse or not enough variety abound, showing evidence that the problem has not been properly addressed yet.

In this section, we will rely on our loss function and a visual inspection of results to assess the quality of our generative model. Later, we will learn other quantitative measures that can be used to guide model training.

Remember that, when analyzing the output of the Generator, it is important to always analyze it with respect to real data so that we know how good fake samples are relative to how good real samples are.

The following is the code:

```
def plot_images(images, filename):
    h, w, c = images.shape[1:]
    grid_size = ceil(np.sqrt(images.shape[0]))
    images = (images.reshape(grid_size, grid_size, h, w, c)
            .transpose(0, 2, 1, 3, 4)
            .reshape(grid_size*h, grid_size*w, c))
    plt.figure(figsize=(16, 16))
    plt.imsave(filename, images)
```

The following function is used to plot the losses from the Discriminator and the Generator. It takes an array with the losses from the Discriminator, the losses from the Generator, and a file path to save the image:

```
def plot_losses(losses_d, losses_g, filename):
    fig, axes = plt.subplots(1, 2, figsize=(8, 2))
    axes[0].plot(losses_d)
    axes[1].plot(losses_g)
    axes[0].set_title("losses_d")
    axes[1].set_title("losses_g")
    plt.tight_layout()
    plt.savefig(filename)
    plt.close()
```

Now that we have defined both auxiliary functions and the models that will be used, let's define our training loop.

Training your GAN

In Chapter 2, *Introduction to Generative Models*, we described GANs as a two-player min-max game, in which the Discriminator and Generator take turns. Informally speaking, the Discriminator learns to identify whether a sample is real or fake while the Generator tries to produce samples that the Discriminator believes to be real.

The implementation of this procedure is, indeed, similar to the informal description. Although, in our first implementation, each model will take one turn at a time, it is possible, and sometimes desirable, to have one model taking more turns than the other.

Our training procedure starts with sampling fake data produced by the Generator and real data. Note that, at this stage, we are not updating the Generator and no gradient is flowing through. Let's start with our method header:

```
def train(ndf=64, ngf=64, z_dim=100, lr_d=2e-4, lr_g=2e-4, epochs=100,
batch_size=128,
          epoch_per_checkpoint=1, n_checkpoint_images=36):
```

Our function header starts with three parameters, ndf , ngf, and z_dim that define the number of Discriminator and Generator filters, and the dimensionality of our latent vector. The next two parameters, lr_d and lr_g, define the learning rate of the Discriminator and the Generator. The remaining parameters are self-descriptive. Let's take a look at the body of the function:

```
X_train, _ = get_data()
image_shape = X_train[0].shape
print("image shape {}, min val {}, max val {}".format(
image_shape, X_train[0].min(), X_train[0].max()))
# plot real images for reference
plot_images(X_train[:n_checkpoint_images], "real_images.png")
```

This excerpt loads our training data, prints the shape of the data, and gives minimum and maximum values for sanity checking. We plot a grid of real images and use it as a reference to evaluate the output of our Generator. Let's now define the computational graphs for our Discriminator and Generator, including the optimizer, loss, and metrics:

```
# build models
D = build_cifar10_discriminator(ndf, image_shape)
G = build_cifar10_generator(ngf, z_dim)

# define Discriminator's optimizer
D.compile(Adam(lr=lr_d, beta_1=0.5), loss='binary_crossentropy',
metrics=['binary_accuracy'])
```

`D` is of a italic and upper case sequential class type, and we use its `compile` method to compile the graph and easily define the optimizer, loss function, and metric of interest. We used the `Adam` optimizer, binary cross entropy loss, as defined in our GAN `loss`, and binary accuracy for metrics. Let's define the computational graph for the Generator now:

```
# define D(G(z)) graph for training the Generator
D.trainable = False
z = Input(shape=(z_dim, ))
D_of_G = Model(inputs=z, outputs=D(G(z)))

# define Generator's Optimizer
D_of_G.compile(Adam(lr=lr_g, beta_1=0.5), loss='binary_crossentropy',
                metrics=['binary_accuracy'])
```

Setting up the Generator's `loss` and metrics requires using the Discriminator, but holding the Discriminator weights fixed. By setting `D. Trainable` to `False`, we can do inference with the Discriminator without weight updates.

After that, we instantiate a `Model` object that can be used to define the computational graph of the Generator outputs going through the Discriminator, `D_of_G`. Notice that the input and output parameters passed to the `Model` class are both symbolic variables that need to be compiled. We compile the `D_of_G` using the `Adam` optimizer, binary cross entropy loss, and binary accuracy as metrics. To compute and store the losses we will need labels and lists respectively. Let's add them to our training method:

```
# get labels for computing the losses
labels_real = np.ones(shape=(batch_size, 1))
labels_fake = np.zeros(shape=(batch_size, 1))
losses_d, losses_g = [], []
```

The original GAN loss requires only real and fake labels. Assuming a fixed batch size, we create labels that will be used when we want to maximize the probability of `real` and minimize the probability of `fake`. The two lists will be used to store our losses during training. Before we start our training loop, let's instantiate a fixed z latent vector such that we can observe the evolution of our images on the fixed z:

```
# fix a z vector for training evaluation
z_fixed = np.random.uniform(-1, 1, size=(n_checkpoint_images, z_dim))
```

In our first implementation, we have sampled the latent vector z from a uniform distribution, which can be visualized as sampling points in a cube in 3D space, as shown in the following diagram:

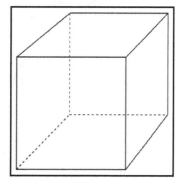

Sampling from a distribution in Python is simple, and can be done with the NumPy library. In the preceding example, we sample a tensor of size `n_checkpoint_images` by `z_dim` from a uniform distribution [-1, 1]. Mathematically, we say $z \sim \mathcal{U}(-1, 1)$. The choice of range of the distribution is based on the *Neural Networks: Tricks of the Trade* paper.

Let's define our training loop now:

```
# training loop
for e in range(epochs):
    print("Epoch {}".format(e))
    for i in range(len(X_train) // batch_size):
```

Our training loop has two levels. The first defines the number of epochs and the second goes over our entire dataset on each epoch, batch by batch. Let's take a look at the Discriminator's turn first:

```
# update Discriminator weights
D.trainable = True
# Get real samples
real_images = X_train[i*batch_size:(i+1)*batch_size]
```

```
loss_d_real = D.train_on_batch(x=real_images, y=labels_real)[0]
# Fake Samples
z = np.random.uniform(-1, 1, size=(batch_size, z_dim))
fake_images = G.predict_on_batch(z)
loss_d_fake = D.train_on_batch(x=fake_images, y=labels_fake)[0]

# Compute Discriminator's loss
loss_d = 0.5 * (loss_d_real + loss_d_fake)
```

During the Discriminator's turn, we want to update its model weights, so we will set its parameter trainable to `True`. The Discriminator's loss has two terms that depend on real and fake data.

We first sample the real data given the current batch, and compute the loss using the real data and the real images.

We then sample the fake data by sampling our `z` latent vector and by using the `predict_on_batch` method, which performs inference while holding the G weights constant. The outputs of G are used to compute the Discriminator's loss. We finally take the average of both losses by multiplying their sum by half.

Let's take a look at the Generator's turn now:

```
# update Generator weights, do not update Discriminator weights
D.trainable = False
loss_g = D_of_G.train_on_batch(x=z, y=labels_real)[0]
```

During the Generator's turn, the weights of D must be held constant, so we have set the Discriminator's trainable parameter to `False`. We use `D_of_G`, to compute the Discriminator's output on fake data and use it to compute the Generator's loss. Note that, in the Generator's turn, no gradients flow into the Discriminator that is held fixed. Now, let's add code to keep track of our losses:

```
losses_d.append(loss_d)
losses_g.append(loss_g)
```

In this implementation, we only keep track of the loss computed on the last iteration of each epoch. We invite you to modify the code and compute the loss at every iteration, and eventually include a moving average to smooth the output.

Finally, we plot the `images` generated by the Generator and the losses:

```
if (e % epoch_per_checkpoint) == 0:
    print("loss_d={:.5f}, loss_g={:.5f}".format(loss_d, loss_g))
    fake_images = G.predict(z_fixed)
    print("\tPlotting images and losses")
```

```
        plot_images(fake_images, "fake_images_e{}.png".format(e))
        plot_losses(losses_d, losses_g, "losses.png")
train()
```

In the following excerpt, we print the Discriminator and Generator losses, predict new fake images from the Generator and plot them using our auxiliary function. After you train the model with the setup and code we provided in this chapter, you should obtain a figure just like this:

Summary

In this chapter, we also learned how to implement our first GAN. We covered some basic theory related to the GAN framework and how it relates to architecture design, especially focusing on the similar capacity of the Discriminator and Generator. We also covered, in detail, the theory behind upsampling layers, weight normalizations, and loss functions seen in GANs.

We learned how to implement the DCGAN Discriminator and Generator architecture, including their optimizers and loss functions. We learned how to implement the training procedure in GANs, wherein the Discriminator and Generator take turns at optimizing their parameters. Finally, we learned how to sample the Generator to get image outputs, and how to visualize those outputs for our amusement and to train the models.

In the next chapter, you will learn how to evaluate your first GAN.

Further reading

The following are topics for further reading:

- The DCGAN Paper
- Image upsampling
- Batch normalization paper or weight normalization summary
- The Convolution Arithmetic Paper

Evaluating Your First GAN

4

The evaluation of **Generative Adversarial Networks** (**GANs**) is a very active and exciting research field in generative models for generative models. Evaluation is the procedure through which we estimate the quality of our model and the samples produced with it. In this chapter, you will learn how to use different methods to evaluate the quality and variety of the GAN samples you produced in `Chapter 3`, *Implementing your First GAN*.

You will learn about the challenges involved in evaluating GAN samples. You will understand and learn to implement metrics for image quality. You will learn about using the birthday paradox to evaluate sample variety.

The following topics will be covered in this chapter:

- The evaluation of GANs
- Qualitative methods
- Quantitative methods
- GANs and the birthday paradox

The evaluation of GANs

The evaluation of GANs is important because it helps us understand what the characteristics of the model we trained are and what we can achieve with it. In this chapter, we will be asking these questions:

- Do the fake samples have an image quality that is similar to the real samples?
- Do the fake samples have a variety that is similar to the real samples?
- Do the fake samples satisfy the specifications of the real samples?

Notice that by asking these questions, we can evaluate our model and specify what we can achieve with it. For example, a model with a low variety in samples, but good image quality, can be used, whereas a model with relatively bad image quality but a good variety produces noisy data that can be used to regularize another model and help it to generalize lower quality images.

Despite its relative youth, several publications (Arjovsky and Bottou, 2017; Salimans et al., 2016; Zhao et al., 2016; and Radford et al., 2015) have investigated the use of the GAN framework for sample generation and unsupervised feature learning.

Unlike other optimization problems in general, where analysis of the empirical risk is a strong indicator of progress, in GANs the decrease in loss does not always correlate with an increase in image quality (Arjovsky et al., 2017), and thus authors still rely on the visual inspection of generated images.

Following the procedure described in Breuleux et al. (2011), and used in Goodfellow et al. (2014), earlier GAN papers evaluated the quality of the fake samples by fitting a Gaussian Parzen window to the fake samples and reporting the log-likelihood of the test set under this distribution.

As mentioned in Goodfellow et al. (2014), this method has some drawbacks, including its high variance and bad performance in high-dimensional spaces. The Inception score is another widely-adopted evaluation metric that fails to provide systematic guidance on the evaluation of GAN models (Barratt and Sharma, 2018).

Fake samples generated with the GANs (Goodfellow et al., 2014) framework have fooled humans and machines to believe that they are indistinguishable from real samples. Although this might be true for the naked eye and the discriminator fooled by the generator, it is unlikely that fake samples are numerically indistinguishable from real samples.

Broadly speaking, current research trends in generative models are focused on increasing the quality of generated samples or enforcing specifications on generated data, estimating what their efficiency is in fooling humans and machines, and understanding the properties of the samples that are produced by them.

Image quality

One important aspect of GAN evaluation is the image quality of the samples produced by the generator relative to the image quality of real samples. A common concern in training GANs is that the images generated by the generator can be blurry. Another concern is that the images can have checkerboard artifacts.

There are both quantitative and qualitative measures for assessing image quality. Whereas traditional quantitative metrics for image quality focus on measures such as distortion and signal to noise ratio, current metrics used in GANs focus on using embeddings obtained from neural networks that have been trained on image classification tasks.

Qualitative measures based on the visual inspection of fake samples can be a quick and dirty mechanism to evaluate image quality. By visualizing a grid of images, we can get the gist of the overall quality of images produced by the generator. This information can be used early on to detect problems with our network.

In the following image, we show fake samples generated with the Progressive Growing of GANs framework, which we will implement later in the book, trained on rock album cover art. Synthesis of rock album covert art with GANs is a project that Aneesh Vartaki and I have been developing recently.

These samples were generated at an intermediary step of the training process where the images start resembling cover art, but still look blurry:

Image variety

Another important aspect of GAN evaluation is image variety. When training GANs, we want to make sure that the Generator is producing varied samples and not just memorizing a few samples. In such cases when the Generator produces only a few images, we . say that the generator is producing only a few modes in the distribution and suffers from mode collapse.

The samples on the image below were generated at an intermediary step of the training process that is later than the step we shared previously. Although the images are considerably less blurry at later iterations, the three red covers seem suspicious. An explanation for these repeated images could be mode collapse, or that the data has a strong bias from images that are repeated multiple times.

The dataset we used to train this model has several identical red cover arts that are similar to the ones shown in the following image. We use this example to illustrate that although repeated images are correlated with mode collapse, there might be confounding factors. In our case, the repeated images were probably caused by a bias in the data that has many repeated images:

Domain specifications

Informally speaking, specifications are deterministic or non-deterministic rules that describe the expected behavior of a system. In music, for example, there are several rules for counterpoint and harmony that describe the expected behavior of a musical style.

While generative models using **Artificial Neural Networks (ANNs)** are extremely powerful, it is not trivial to predict the outcome given the input, especially in situations where the output of the system is recursively used as the input. On the other hand, models based on automata are more predictable, but usually, they lack the power and flexibility of ANNs.

A formal specification is a mathematical statement of what a system must or must not do, often expressed in mathematical logic or using automata-theoretic formalisms. Although there has been work on combining neural networks and control, there are many challenges related to verified artificial intelligence that are yet to be solved.

In the following image, we show fake samples generated with the Progressive GAN framework, which we will implement later in the book, trained on rock album cover art. These samples were generated at an intermediary step of the training process that is later than the step we shared previously. A visual inspection of the samples shows that, broadly speaking, these fake images partially satisfy specifications that we can associate with cover art.

The specifications of rock album cover art can include the following:

- The band name or album title on the bottom or top of cover art
- The band name and album title close to each other
- Objects at the center of the image
- The extensive use of black
- Abstract objects without a band name or album title

Through a visual inspection of these samples, it is clear that what is intended to resemble features such as a band name or album title does not resemble the Latin alphabet, for example, which is so common in cover art. In addition, the objects on the cover art, albeit aesthetically interesting, do not resemble concrete objects:

In the following image, we provide real images of rock album cover art:

Qualitative methods

The evaluation of GANs with qualitative methods focuses on exploratory data analysis. In such methods, the researcher evaluates the fake samples by visual inspection. This can be done independently from other samples or with respect to real samples. Qualitative methods are useful as they can quickly provide information about issues with your current GAN experiment related to image quality, image variety, and the violation of specifications.

In GAN literature, the visual inspection of samples is a very common practice and authors use it to quickly confirm that they have not observed mode collapse or that their framework is robust to mode collapse if some criteria is met (Arjovsky et al., 2017; Gulrajani et al., 2017; Mao et al., 2016; and Radford et al., 2015).

Qualitative methods for evaluation are very useful to quickly detect problems with fake data. This allows us to quickly modify our experiment to achieve better results. This qualitative evaluation, however, comes at the price of being superficial and not systematic. For a deeper and more systematic evaluation of fake samples, it is necessary to devise a systematic, quantitative evaluation.

In the following sections, we provide some qualitative measures for GAN evaluation, as elaborated by Ali Borji in his paper, *Pros and Cons of GAN Evaluation Measures*.

k-nearest neighbors

Generally speaking, the k-nearest neighbors algorithm is a non-parametric technique that given samples n in a dataset ($\mathcal{N}$), reference samples (r), and some similarity measures (S), k-nearest neighbors finds the k samples in $\mathcal{N}$ most similar to r, given S. Assuming that samples are represented as points in some space, the closest point to a reference point can be thought of as its neighbor.

Mathematically speaking, k-nearest neighbors can be defined as follows:

$$n^* = \arg\max_{n \in \mathcal{N}} S(n, r)$$

Note that we can trivially use a distance measure, D, instead of a similarity measure and find the closest samples:

$$n^* = \arg\min_{n \in \mathcal{N}} D(n, r)$$

A naive implementation of the k-nearest neighbors algorithm is simple with NumPy. It consists of computing the similarity or distance between the reference, r, and the samples, n, in N, and then finding the index of the largest k similarities or smallest k distances. In the following implementation, we find the smallest k distances:

```
# get the training data D, sample the Generator with random z to produce r
N = X_train
z = np.random.uniform(-1, 1, (1, z_dim))
r = G.predict_on_batch(z)

# define our distance measure S to be L1
S = lambda n, r: np.sum(np.abs(n - r))

# compute the distances between the reference and the samples in N using
the measure D
distances = [D(n, r) for n in N]

# find the indices of the most similar samples and select them from N
nearest_neighbors_index = np.argpartition(distances, k)
nearest_neighbors_images = N[nearest_neighbors_index]
```

In the context of the qualitative evaluation of GANs, k-nearest neighbors can be used to detect overfitting. This is done by sampling fake samples from the generator, using k-nearest neighbors to find their most similar samples in the training set, and plotting the images side-by-side for visual inspection. In the following image, we provide one example found in the appendix of the paper, *Progressive Growing of GANs for Improved Quality, Stability, and Variation*:

Source: Progressive Growing of GANs for Improved Quality, Stability, and Variation
(https://arxiv.org/abs/1710.10196)

The images on the top were generated by GANs. The images on the bottom are their nearest neighbors in the training set given the L1 distance in pixel space. Visual inspection quickly shows that the nearest neighbors are similar, but not equal, to the reference sample. This is preliminary evidence that the generator is not overfitting the training set.

Mode analysis

When using datasets with known modes (such as a Gaussian mixture model or a labeled dataset), we can easily evaluate the fake samples for mode collapse and mode drop. In GANs, mode collapse loosely refers to the lack of diversity in generated samples, and mode drop refers to the absence of a mode that exists in the training data but does not exist in the generator data.

For example, when trained on a multimodal distribution such as MNIST, a dataset of handwritten digits with 10 modes, each representing a digit, the samples produced by the generator might not include all the modes of the distribution and drop some of the digits.

In this context, mode analysis is done by sampling fake images from the generator, plotting them, and looking for mode drops. In the following diagram, we provide a fictitious example of mode collapse on the MNIST dataset, where half the modes are missing:

Fictitious fake samples produced by a GAN. Several modes of the distribution are missing (5, 6, 7, 8, and 9).

Other methods

There are other methods that include setting up experiments and asking participants to evaluate images or visualize the network. For experiments with participants, it is important to remember that the setup of the experiment might be different from the use case. For example, experiments that require participants to quickly make a judgment are probably different from the context in which these images will be used.

- **Rapid Scene Categorization**: As the name suggests, in rapid scene categorization experiments, the participants are asked to distinguish between real and fake samples under a short time constraint, for example, 100 ms.
- **Ranking**: As the name suggests, in ranking, participants are asked to rank images according to some criteria described by the investigator. In these experiments, the images can be ranked independently, such as **Mean Opinion Scores** (**MOS**), or with respect to other images.
- **Network Visualization**: This technique takes advantage of(such as space continuity) as well as visualizing learned features.

Quantitative methods

The objective function used in GANs is a quantitative measure that provides information about each player's performance, discriminator, and generator in the GAN game. For example, in the first GAN objective function, the output of the discriminator on fake data provides information about how well the generator is fooling the discriminator and how well the discriminator can identify real data. Although this information is useful because it provides information about the status of the minimax game and how close it is to equilibrium, it provides absolutely no information about the images themselves.

In this context, researchers in the GAN community have been developing quantitative methods that can be used to measure image quality, variety, and satisfaction of specifications.

In this section, we will address a few of such measures, including the following:

- The Inception score
- The Frechét Inception score
- Precision, Recall, and the F1 score

The Inception score

The Inception score is a heuristics-based method to measure the quality and diversity of fake images. The score uses a pretrained neural network for image classification, called the Inception network. It was first proposed in the paper, *Improved Techniques for Training GANs*.

The main novelties in Inception networks are the addition of 1 x 1 convolution layers and the global average pooling layers with multiple convolutions (1 x 1, 3 x 3, and 5 x 5), and a 3 x 3 max pooling layer.

Whereas the 1 x 1 convolution layers are a weighted combination of all the input channels at the current layer, the global average pooling layer improves the robustness of spatial translation and replaces dense layers, thus decreasing the number of parameters in the model but achieving better results.

 You can read a valuable introduction to Inception networks, available at https://towardsdatascience.com/a-simple-guide-to-the-versions-of-the-inception-network-7fc52b863202.

To compute the Inception score, we generate thousands of fake images, feed them through the Inception network that was trained for image classification, and analyze the softmax logits output by the network.

- **Image Quality**: Under the assumption that the Inception network will have low entropy outputs when provided with images that come from the true distribution of the data it was trained on, e. g. unimodal output showing high probability for a single class, the entropy of the outputs of the Inception network on fake data can be used as a proxy for fake data image quality.
- **Image Variety**: Under the assumption that the fake samples come from the same true distribution of the data that the Inception network was trained on, and that the Inception network has a high level of accuracy in its predictions, we can compare the distribution of labels on the real data to the distribution of labels on the fake data to evaluate class variety. Note that this does not imply that there is variety within each class.

These two criteria are combined and the Inception score is represented in the following equation:

$$IS(G) = \exp \mathbb{E}_{\hat{x} \sim p_g} D_{KL}(p(y \mid \hat{x}) \parallel p(y)),$$

Here, $\hat{x} \sim P_g$ are fake images sampled from the generator, P_g. The $P(y)$ term computes the marginal distribution of the class label's y output by the Inception model, fix position of $p(y \mid \hat{x})$ term computes the conditional distribution of the class labels given the $\hat{x}$ images sampled from the generator, P_g. Remember from Chapter 2, *An Introduction to Generative Models*, the equation for the KL divergence between two continuous distributions is as follows:

$$D_{KL}(P \parallel Q) = \int_{-\infty}^{+\infty} p(x) \log \frac{q(x)}{p(x)} dx$$

In our case, $p(y|x)$ and $p(y)$ are distributions computed over a discrete support that represents the class labels. In the discrete form, the KL divergence becomes the following:

$$D_{KL}(P \parallel Q) = -\sum_i p(x_i) \log \frac{q(x_i)}{p(x_i)}$$

Most implementations, however, swap the terms in the log difference and remove the negative sign, obtaining the same result:

$$D_{KL}(P \parallel Q) = \sum_i p(x_i) \log \frac{p(x_i)}{q(x_i)}$$

Literally, this is the expectation, computed using probabilities, P, of the logarithmic differences between Q and P. In the Inception score, $p(x_i)$ P represents $p(y_i \mid \hat{x}_i)$, and Q represents $p(y_i)$. The Inception score becomes the following:

$$IS(G) = \sum_i p(y \mid \hat{x}) \log \frac{p(y \mid \hat{x})}{q(y)}$$

Note that in the equation, we referred to the generator, but conveniently did not refer to the Inception network being used. It is important to understand that the Inception score is not independent of the Inception network and will change if you use a different Inception network.

Now that we have presented the Inception score mathematically, implementing it becomes a matter of translating math into code. We compute $p(y \mid \hat{x})$ by sampling fake images from the generator, passing them through the Inception network, and collecting their outputs. Note that the Inception score is not GANs specific and can be computed on any data. Let's start by generating some data:

```
# generate fake images from the discriminator
n_fake_images = 5000
z = np.random.uniform(-1, 1, (n_fake_images, z_dim))
x = G.predict_on_batch(z)
```

Now let's define the method that computes the Inception score:

```
def compute_inception_score(x, inception_model, n_fake_images, z_dim):
    # probability of y given x
    p_y_given_x = inception_model.predict_on_batch(x)
```

We compute $q(y)$ by marginalizing the Inception network's output label distribution on fake samples:

```
    # marginal probability of y
q_y = np.mean(p_y_given_x, axis=0)
```

Now, we can finally compute the Inception score of our generator:

```
    inception_scores = p_y_given_x * (np.log(p_y_given_x) - np.log(q_y)
    inception_score = np.exp(np.mean(inception_scores))
    return inception_score
```

In the original proposal, the authors suggested computing the Inception score 10 times with N = 5,000, and then averaging over the scores and taking the standard deviation. For more details, you can read the Inception score paper.

The Frechét Inception Distance

The **Fréchet Inception Distance** (**FID**) was proposed by Martin Heusel et al., in their paper, *GANs Trained by a Two Time-Scale Update Rule Converge to a Local Nash Equilibrium*, as an alternative to the Inception score. One of the drawbacks of the Inception score is that it is a discriminative model; in other words, the Inception network is not robust to adversarial examples and can output high confidence on such adversarial examples. In their paper, the proposed solution to this problem is to compare the statistics of real samples with generated samples.

Similar to the Inception score, FID uses a pretrained Inception network. The FID is a distance measure between the means (μ_r, μ_g) and covariance matrices (Σ_r, Σ_g) of the activations from an intermediate layer of an Inception network computed on real and generated data, respectively. Note that by computing the means and covariances, the FID is fitting a multivariate Gaussian to the activations. The FID between the real images, x, and generated images, g, is defined as follows:

$$FID(x, g) = \| \mu_r - \mu_g \|_2^2 + Tr(\Sigma_r + \Sigma_g - 2(\Sigma_r \Sigma_g)^{\frac{1}{2}}),$$

Here, we parametrize $X_r \sim N(\mu_r, \Sigma_r), X_g \sim (\mu_g, \Sigma_g)$ and Tr represents the trace of a matrix; that is, the sum of all diagonal elements.

The FID can be used to detect a low variety within each mode of the distribution of images produced by the generator. While the Inception score will be high for generators that, for example, output one sample per mode but lack within the mode variety, the score will be low, that is, a large distance, for the FID.

The code for parametrizing the activations with a normal distribution is simple; we compute the means and covariance matrices on the activations of real and generated data. Let's take a look at a naive implementation:

```
def get_mean_and_covariance(data):
    mean = np.mean(data, axis=0)
    covariance = np.cov(data, rowvar=False) # rowvar?
    return mean, covariance
```

With these statistics in hand, we implement the FID defined in the preceding equation as follows:

```
def compute_frechet_inception_distance(mean_r, mean_f, cov_r, cov_f):
    l2_mean = np.sum((mean_r - mean_f)**2)
    cov_mean, _ = np.trace(scipy.linalg.sqrtm(np.dot(cov_r, cov_f)))
    return l2_mu + np.trace(cov_r) + np.trace(cov_f) - 2 *
np.trace(cov_mean)
```

Precision, Recall, and the F1 Score

Precision, recall, and the F1 Score are metrics related to classification. Precision is the ratio of true positives to true positives plus false positives; in other words, given the items that the model identified as positives, the number of these that are correctly positive. Recall is the ratio of true positives to true positives plus false negatives. In other words, given the items that the model has recognized and not recognized, the number that are recognized. The F1 score is the harmonic average of Precision and recall:

- **Precision**: TP / TP + FP
- **Pecall**: TP / TP + FN
- **F1 scores**: 2 (Precision * Recall) / Precision + Recall

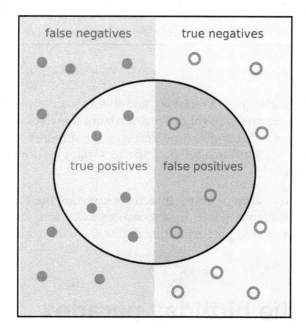

A famous image used to illustrate Precision and recall. Source: Wikipedia (https://en.wikipedia.org/wiki/Precision_and_recall)

In the Google Brain research paper, *Are GANs Created Equal ?*, a toy experiment with a dataset of triangles at different scales and rotations is created to measure the Precision and the recall of different GANs. The following diagram from the paper explains how Precision and recall are used to evaluate GANs:

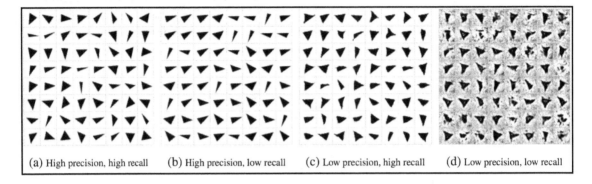

(a) High precision, high recall   (b) High precision, low recall   (c) Low precision, high recall   (d) Low precision, low recall

Source: Are GANs Created Equal? (https://arxiv.org/abs/1711.10337)

In (a), all images are triangles (high Precision), and there's a variety of triangles (high recall); in (b), all images are triangles (high Precision), but they lack variety (low recall); in (c), most images are imperfect triangles (low Precision), and there's a variety in size and rotation (high recall). In (d), most images are imperfect triangles (low Precision), and there's little variety (low recall).

Note that computing these scores requires directly computing the variety and quality of the samples being evaluated. Hence, while these measures work well with simple geometric shapes, it is hard to quantify the properties that define the variety and quality of the samples.

GANs and the birthday paradox

One of the biggest challenges in evaluating GANs samples is to understand how much of the real distribution the generator has learned. For example, let's consider the size of the support for the set of all the possible images of dogs. Naturally, this set must include millions of dog images that portray combinations of all dog features, including size, breed, hair color, pose, and more.

Assuming there are millions of dogs in real life that we humans perceive as unique, a GAN that has truly learned the distribution of dogs must be able to produce a similar number of unique dog images. Estimating the number of unique images of dogs a GAN is able to produce might seem like a daunting task at first, but researchers have found a brilliant crude estimate of this by using the birthday paradox.

The birthday paradox is commonly addressed in undergraduate classes where teachers ask students in the class what the probability is that two people in the class have the same birthday. After some speculation, students are normally dazzled to find out that even with only 23 people in a room, the chances that two of them have the same birthday is about 50%. With 23 people in a room, there are $23 * 22/2$ unique unordered pairs. We divide by 2 because the order does not matter. The probability that people in a pair have a different birthday is $364/365$. Hence, the probability that none of the unique unordered pairs represent a match in birthday is equal to $(364/365)^{253}$, which is approximately 50%.

The birthday paradox says that in a discrete distribution of support, N, a random sample of size $\sqrt{N}$ is likely to have a duplicate. GANs have continuous support and, therefore, some intervention is needed to adapt the birthday paradox to the GAN framework.

A simple yet efficient intervention is to use some image similarity measure to detect a collision and then, given a sample image, use the number of similar images to identify the size of the support of the distribution. Naturally, this method is dependent on the image similarity measure. Normally, two images are considered similar if the distances between them is within some epsilon. This epsilon parameter directly influences the number of collisions that will be found.

The birthday paradox test for GANs proposed by Sanjeev Aurora, is as follows:

1. Pick a sample S of size n, produced with the generator.
2. Use some similarity measure to compute the similarity between the images in S.
3. Flag the 20 (say) most similar pairs in the sample.
4. Visually inspect the flagged images for near duplicates.
5. Repeat the process.

After running this experiment several times, we gather information about how likely it is to find near duplicates in the sample, S. If the samples of size n have duplicates with good probability, we'd suspect that the distribution has a support size of about n^2.

The birthday paradox works for GANs, especially under the assumption that the generator applies uniform probability to images in its distributions. In cases where the probability distribution is not uniform, the birthday paradox fails.

The following image is from the paper, *Do GANs Actually Learn the Distribution? An Empirical Study.* In the first and second column, authors show the most similar pairs found in batches of 640 generated faces samples from a DCGAN. The third column shows the nearest neighbors in training data; each pair is from a different batch:

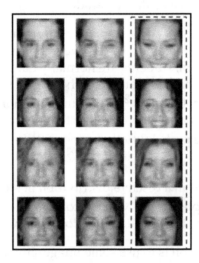

Source: Do GANs Actually Learn the Distribution? An Empirical Study (https://arxiv.org/abs/1706.08224)

 For more information about the birthday paradox, refer to Sanjeev Aurora's excellent paper and blog post, available at http://www. offconvex.org/2017/07/06/GANs3/.

Summary

In this chapter, we learned how to evaluate GANS, and this helped us to understand the various characteristics of the model. We also covered GAN with qualitative and quantitative methods and learned about their differences. Finally, we learned how to adapt the birthday paradox to the GAN framework.

In the next chapter, we will see how to solve the major challenges that arise in training and understanding GANs.

Improving Your First GAN

In this chapter, you will learn about the main challenges in training and understanding **Generative Adversarial Networks (GANs)**, as well as how to solve them. You will learn about vanishing gradients, mode collapse, training instability, and other challenges. You will also learn about multiple deep-learning model architectures that have been successful using the GAN framework. Furthermore, you will learn to possibly improve your first GAN by implementing new loss functions and algorithms.

In this chapter we will continue to focus on the CIFAR-10 dataset and cover the following topics:

- Challenges in training GANs
- Tricks of the trade
- GAN model architectures
- GAN algorithms and loss functions

Technical requirements

You can find the code files for this chapter at the following GitHub link: `https://github.com/PacktPublishing/Hands-On-Generative-Adversarial-Networks-with-Keras`

Challenges in training GANs

The challenges mentioned in this section relate to training GANs which can have the following major problems:

- Mode collapse and mode drop
- Training instability

- Sensitivity to hyperparameter initialization
- Vanishing gradients

Let's now move on and address each of these problems individually.

Mode collapse and mode drop

Mode collapse and mode drop are common problems in GANs. They refer to reduced variety in the samples produced by a generator. The term has been used interchangeably and has the following two main interpretations:

1. The generator synthesizes samples with intra-mode variety, but some modes are missing.
2. The generator synthesizes samples with inter-mode variety, but each mode lacks variety.

Note that both the first and the second interpretation assume that a model has high precision and low recall. The first interpretation refers to low inter-mode recall, that is, when there is a variety in the modes present in the synthesized samples but not all modes are present; the second interpretation refers to low intra-mode recall, that is, all modes are present, but within each mode the synthesized samples lack variety.

Research and hacks into how to circumvent mode collapse and mode drop in GANs have been developed in recent years. Common hacks to circumvent these problems include training one generator per mode of the distribution, or using a weighted sampling scheme to sample the real data, such that modes that appear infrequently in the samples produced by the generator are sampled more often.

There are also solutions that consist of using an objective function that is different from the original GAN objective, which compares distributions from real and fake data with a different distance. The Least Squares GAN uses a least squares distance, the Wasserstein GAN uses the Wasserstein distance, energy-based GANs use total-variation distance, and the Relativistic GAN uses a log-odds distance. We will address some of these objective functions later on in this chapter.

In addition, there is a solution that consists of updating the discriminator for more iterations than the generator. This solution is based on the belief that, by doing so, the discriminator has access to a larger pool of samples, meaning the generator will no longer overfit to the current sample. It is also believed that by doing multiple discriminator updates, the generator has indirect access to the trajectory of future discriminator updates.

Note that these strategies are substantially empirical and their success is most commonly the result of trial and error.

Training instability

Training instability refers to the weight updates that occur in the GAN optimization process. It is believed that a few factors contribute to instability in weight updates, including:

- Sparse gradients
- Disjoint support between fake images and real images

Non-linearities such as ReLU and Max Pooling produce sparse gradients that can make training unstable. We will propose solutions in this chapter on how to avoid sparse gradients in GANs. For now, let's investigate disjoint support.

In the original GAN setup, we optimize the discriminator by learning a decision boundary that separates real data from fake data. If the support of the fake images does not overlap with the real images, the discriminator can perfectly differentiate between what is real and what is fake. This property breaks the assumptions in the GAN loss in multiple ways. To understand this, let's start by visualizing an image of two non-overlapping distributions, as provided in the paper *Amortised Map Inference for Image Super-Resolution* by Casper Kaae Sønderby, which proposes a solution to instability in GANs. Take a look at the following diagram:

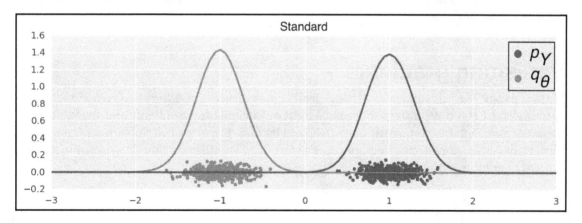

Source: Amortised Map Inference for Image Super-Resolution (https://arxiv.org/abs/1610.04490)

In the preceding diagram, the blue points represent real data, the red points represent fake data, and they were both sampled from two Gaussian distributions. The distribution of fake data learned by the generator $W \, p_Y \, W$. The distribution of real data with latent parameters ψ is represented as P_Y. A few interesting things happen when the distributions q_θ and p_ϕ are disjoint and perfectly separable, such as:

- The KL divergence is not well-defined.
- The JS divergence is saturated and locally constant due to multiple near-optimal solutions.
- The multiple near-optimal solutions may be highly-dependent on initialization and could even provide very different gradients.

A possibly effective solution for disjoint distributions between q_θ and p_ϕ is to add limited noise to real images. This technique is called **Instance Noise** and will be explained later on in this chapter, in the section about adding noise to the GAN setup.

Sensitivity to hyperparameter initialization

In their paper *Are GANs Created Equal? A Large-Scale Study*, researchers at Google Brain did a large-scale study in which multiple GAN losses with different hyperparameter initializations were evaluated under multiple evaluation measures. In this study, they found that most models can reach similar scores with enough hyperparameter optimization and random restarts. This suggests that most models are very sensitive to hyperparameter initialization, and that improvements can arise from computational budgeting and tuning rather than algorithmic changes.

Vanishing gradients

In their paper *Towards Principled Methods for Training Generative Adversarial Networks*, Martin Ajovsky and Léon Bottou shed theoretical light onto vanishing gradients and unstable behavior associated with the original GAN and its loss. Here, we briefly summarize a few important conclusions from the paper. Let's start by remembering that the discriminator is trained to maximize the following:

$$\mathbb{E}_{x \sim \mathbb{P}_r}\left[log \, D(x)\right] + \mathbb{E}_{z \sim \mathbb{P}_z}\left[log\left(1 - D(g_\theta(z))\right)\right]$$

When trained until convergence, the loss of the discriminator will be minimized be when $D(x) = 1$ for real samples $x \sim \mathbb{P}_r$ and $D(x) = 0$ for fake samples $z \sim \mathbb{P}_z$. This is only possible when two distributions are completely separable, which happens only if the distributions have disjoint supports or if the distribution are not continuous.

In the case of convergence, the optimal discriminator is perfect and its gradient will be zero almost everywhere. This can be a problem: as the discriminator approaches during training an optimal discriminator, the gradients start to vanish, preventing any significant weight updates.

To avoid this problem, a different gradient step has been chosen for the generator, as follows:

$$\Delta\theta = \nabla_\theta \mathbb{E}_{z\sim p(z)}\left[-\log D(g_\theta(z))\right]$$

Unfortunately, given the correct assumptions, each coordinate of this expectation is a centered Cauchy distribution with infinite expectation and variance. Therefore, this property can lead to unstable updates.

In this chapter, we are going to describe a few loss functions that attempt to circumvent the issues we've discussed at the cost of introducing other issues.

Tricks of the trade

In this section, we will provide an extensive list of tricks compiled from the GAN research community, from Soumith Chintala in particular. The following list can help with the notably hard task of training GANs. Compared to MLE approaches that have been implemented and evaluated for decades, and are also much simpler to train, the GAN framework is only a few years old. There are many developments that been made, therefore, that improve the evaluation and training procedure.

Tracking failure

It is important to track failure early on to speed up the training process.

Loss of the discriminator goes to 0.

When the loss of the discriminator goes to 0, as mentioned, the updates of the generator are insignificant.

Check the norm of the gradients.

When the norm of the gradients is large, it means relatively large weight updates. Although this is expected on the first iterations, the norm should decrease as training proceeds.

Check the variance over time of the Discriminator's Loss.

It is expected that the variance of the discriminator's loss decreases over time and does not have sudden spikes.

Working with labels

Train the discriminator to classify using the labels and the generator to synthesize conditioned on the labels.

There is a belief that training the discriminator to classify samples and then providing labels as input to the generator can, in turn, improve GAN training. When successful, this setup also allows us to provide a label to the generator to sample from a specific mode of the distribution.

Working with discrete inputs

Use an embedding layer with discrete inputs.

An embedding layer learns a projection from discrete inputs into a dense vector of fixed size. This has several advantages, including the following:

- The network learns the best embedding given the task at hand.
- The dimensionality of the discrete input can be reduced.

Learn discrete input upsampling to match image channel size.

It is believed that it is better to keep the embedding dimensionality low and upsample it to match the image channel size at the layer at hand.

Concatenate discrete inputs with image channels.

In theory, concatenating discrete inputs with images over the channel's dimension and then applying a convolution or dense layer is a superset of adding or multiplying the embedded discrete inputs with the images directly. Hence, concatenating is theoretically preferred because it has more capacity.

In practice, concatenating can be harder to optimize, so it is preferable to try adding or multiplying discrete inputs with images directly.

Adding noise

It is reported that adding noise to the training procedure can improve training because it makes the support of the real and fake distributions less separable, thus potentially eliminating vanishing gradients and training instabilities. Take a look at the following list of some of these strategies:

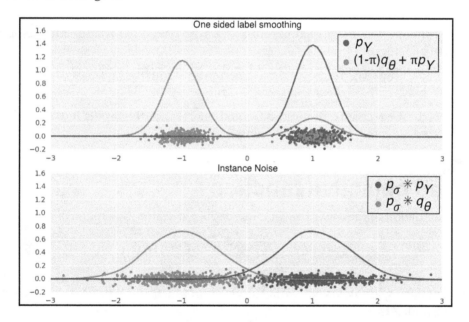

Source: Amortised MAP inference for Image Super-Resolution (https://arxiv.org/abs/1610.04490)

- Flip labels occasionally: By flipping labels occasionally, real becomes fake and fake becomes real. The preceding diagram shows the effect on a multivariate-Gaussian distribution with two modes. Note that flipping the labels does not create an overlap between the supports of the distributions.

- Use label smoothing: Alter the labels so that they are close to 0 and 1 but not exactly 0 and 1. This can be done by randomly adding small numbers to the fake label 0 and randomly subtracting small numbers to the real label.
- Add noise to the input data: Adding uniform noise to the input data can help create an overlap between the support of the real distribution and the fake distribution, as demonstrated in the preceding diagram. Normally, the amount of noise added decays over time.
- Add noise in the form of dropout: When training conditional GANs, adding 50% dropout to the generator can help. This strategy has been used in the *Image-to-Image Translation with Conditional Adversarial Networks* paper by Philip Isola et al.

Input normalization

We have two cases of normalization:

- Normalize the images between 0 and 1, where Sigmoid is added to the output of the generator.
- Normalize the images between -1 and 1, where Tanh is added to the output of the generator

In both cases, these preceding alterations not only normalize the inputs but also make their ranges bounded, which is helpful for training.

Modified objective function

The first formulation of the objective function of the generator is as follows:

$$\min_{G} \mathbb{E}_{z \sim p_z} [log(1 - D(G(z)))]$$

It includes vanishing gradients early on. However, in practice, it's preferable to use the following formula:

$$\max_{G} \mathbb{E}_{z \sim p_z} [logD(G(z))]$$

Note that this objective function, as we described earlier, can produce unstable updates.

Distribute latent vector Z

In his paper *Sampling Generative Networks*, Tom White claims that sampling z from a spherical distribution prevents diverging from a model's prior distribution and produces sharper samples. The guidelines are as follows:

> Do not sample from a uniform distribution; sample from a spherical distribution.

Sampling a spherical distribution in `keras` is simple and is equal to sampling a normal distribution, as follows:

```
z = keras.random_normal(0, 1, z_dim)
```

Weight normalization

> When batch norm is not an option, use instance normalization (for each sample, subtract mean and divide by standard deviation.)

Instance normalization normalizes the activation of a neural network layer by subtracting it by its mean and dividing it by its standard deviation. This operation is done per channel.

Avoid sparse gradients

> Use LeakyReLU in generator and discriminator.

Training GANs is already an unstable task and using non-linearities such as ReLU will produce sparse gradients that can make the instability worse.

Use a different optimizer

> Use adaptive learning methods such as ADAM or RMSProp.

We have already evaluated and proposed solutions to the instability of training GANs. If these proposed solutions fail, there's always the option of using different optimizers. Empirically, training GANs with ADAM seems to yield better samples.

Learning rate schedule

Choose learning rates according to the problem at hand.

One of the challenges in training neural networks is setting the proper learning rate. Within the GAN framework, wherein one looks for an equilibrium between the discriminator and the generator networks, this challenge gets exacerbated given the presence of a learning rate for each network and the dependencies between losses.

For discriminator and generator networks of equal size, one expects the discriminator to have some advantage over the generator such that the updates provided by the discriminator to the generator are useful. This can be achieved by setting the discriminator's learning rate to be slightly higher than the generator, or by performing more discriminator updates than generator updates.

For discriminator and generator networks where the generator is larger than the discriminator, the strategy can differ. For example, let's consider a context-encoder generator as the one described in [104]. In this example, the generator has more parameters than the discriminator given that it has both an encoder that interprets the context and a decoder that generates the missing data. In this case, the training process of the generator is slower and the balance between discriminator and generator can be disrupted if the learning rates are the same.

GAN model architectures

The following section will discuss alternative GAN model architectures for the Discriminator and Generator.

ResNet GAN

In its simplest form, a ResNet network is a network with residual layers. A residual layer is a layer in which the layer input is added to the layer output. This connection from the layer input to the layer output is called a residual connection, as illustrated in the following diagram:

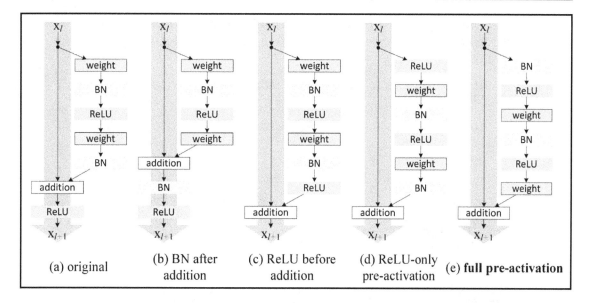

Multiple variations of the a ResNet layer. Copied from *Identity Mappings in Deep Residual Networks* (https://arxiv.org/abs/1603.05027)

Let's take a look at an implementation of a ResNet GAN that could be used for image denoising, image super resolution, image-to-image translation, audio denoising amongst many other tasks. This ResNet GAN takes in an image as input and produces another image as output.

In Keras, it is simple to implement a residual block. In the following code, we provide an example of an implementation of the original ResNet block show in the figure above. We assume the necessary classes and methods are already imported.

```
def ResnetBlock(inputs, n_filters):
    # 'same' padding to keep tensor size fixed
    x = Conv2D(filters=n_filters, kernel_size=(3, 3),
padding='same')(inputs)
    x = BatchNormalization()(x)
    x = Activation('relu')(x)

    # 'same' padding to keep tensor size fixed
    x = Conv2D(filters=n_filters, kernel_size=(3, 3), padding='same')(x)
    x = BatchNormalization()(x)
    # additive residual connection, tensors must have the same size
    output = Add()([inputs, x])
    output = Activation('relu')(output)
    return output
```

Assuming the necessary imports have been added, an encoder-decoder ResNet `Generator` can be implemented as in the code-block below. We assume the necessary classes and methods are already imported.

```python
def Generator(input_shape, n_channels, ngf, n_encoding_blocks,
n_resnet_blocks,
                n_decoding_blocks):
    # apply convolution front-end to inputs
    inputs = Input(shape=input_shape)
    x = Conv2D(filters=ngf, kernel_size=(3, 3), padding='same')(inputs)
    x = BatchNormalization()(x)
    x = Activation('relu')(x)
    # encoder: increase number filters and decrease image dimension by a
factor of 2
    for i in range(n_encoding_blocks):
        x = Conv2D(filters=ngf * 2 ** i, kernel_size=(3, 3), strides=2,
padding='same')(x)
        x = BatchNormalization()(x)
        x = Activation('relu')(x)
    # resnet blocks, keep number of filters and dimensionality the same
    for i in range(n_resnet_blocks):
        x = ResnetBlock(x, ngf * 2 ** (n_encoding_blocks-1))
    # decoder: decrease number filters and increase image dimension by a
factor of 2
    for i in range(n_decoding_blocks-1, -1, -1):
        x = Conv2DTranspose(filters=int(ngf * 2 ** i), kernel_size=(3,3),
strides=2,
                            padding='same')(x)
        x = BatchNormalization()(x)
        x = Activation('relu')(x)

    x = Conv2D(filters=n_channels, kernel_size=(3, 3), padding='same')(x)
    # assumes input image is in the [-1, 1] range,
    x = Activation('tanh')(x)

    # add additive residual connection from input to output
    outputs = Add()([x, inputs])

    # x + inputs can be [-2, 2]. scale to [-1, 1] by dividing by 2
    outputs = Lambda(lambda z: z/2)(outputs)
    model = Model(inputs=inputs, outputs=x, name='Generator')
    return model
```

The `Discriminator` can be implemented as follows:

```python
def Discriminator(input_shape, ndf, n_resnet_blocks):
    inputs = Input(shape=input_shape)
```

```
# project to ndf
x = Conv2D(filters=ngf, kernel_size=(1, 1), padding='same')(inputs)
# resnet blocks, increase dimension by a factor of 2 per iteration
for i in range(n_resnet_blocks):
    x = ResnetBlock(x, ngf, resample='down')
# project to single width and height
x = Conv2D(filters=ngf, kernel_size=(4, 4), padding='valid')(x)

# use dense layer to project to single channel and reshape
x = Dense(1)(x)
x = Reshape((1, ))(x)
x = Activation('sigmoid')(x)
model = Model(inputs=inputs, outputs=x, name='Discriminator')
return model
```

GAN algorithms and loss functions

Similar to tricks for training neural networks, there are a few sources that provide best practices for training generative adversarial networks. These best practices were mainly developed to circumvent the difficulty in training GANs using the objective function described in 2.4. Note that these tricks might not apply nor be necessary to other GAN formulations such as LSGAN or WGAN.

Some of the problems associated with the original GAN objective function seem to have been addressed with the development of relativistic loss functions like the Least-Squares GAN (LSGAN) and the Wasserstein GAN (WGAN).

We present these different algorithms and loss functions, recommending that you study them in tandem with Google's recent research in *Are GANs Created Equal*. In this paper, while referring to different GAN loss functions and algorithms, the authors claim that they did not find evidence that any of the tested algorithms consistently outperform the original.

Naturally, the claims made in the paper *Are GANs Created Equal* only apply to the experimental setup in the paper. In other experimental setups, it is possible that a loss function and algorithm consistently outperforms the standard GAN.

Nonetheless, the paper shows evidence that GANs are very sensitive to hyperparameter initialization. Hence, we suggest the reader to not prematurely switch between GAN frameworks and losses: instead, start from hyperparameters that are known to work and only then do a hyperparameter search.

Last, all these suggestions operate under the *not always true* assumption that the code we are running has no bugs. Thus, we suggest the reader to first ensure that this assumption holds and that there are no bugs in the code before prematurely looking into other areas of improvement.

 For more information on the paper *Are GANs Created Equal*, you can visit the following link: https://medium.com/@jonathan_hui/gan-does-lsgan-wgan-wgan-gp-or-began-matter-e19337773233.

Least Squares GAN

The Least Squares GAN uses the least squares objective function to train the discriminator and generator. Unlike the Sigmoid Cross Entropy, the Least Squares loss more heavily penalizes samples regarding their position with respect to the decision boundary. In their paper, the authors affirm that the LSGAN contributes to the stability of the learning process, removes the need of using batch normalization, and converges faster than the Wasserstein GAN.

The objective functions of LSGAN for the discriminator D and generator G are the following:

$$\min_{D} L_{LSGAN}(D) = \frac{1}{2}\mathbb{E}_{x\sim p_r}[(D(x) - b)^2] + \frac{1}{2}\mathbb{E}_{z\sim p_z(z)}[(D(G(z)) - a)^2]$$

$$\min_{G} L_{LSGAN}(G) = \frac{1}{2}\mathbb{E}_{z\sim p_r}[(D(G(z)) - c)^2$$

The authors of LSGAN state that, with specific relationships between a, b, and c values, minimizing this loss is equal to minimizing Pearson X2 divergence. The specific a, b, and c relationships are $b - c = 1$ and $b - a = 2$. This can be achieved by setting $a = -1, b = 1$ and $c = 0$, for example:

$$\min_{D} L_{LSGAN}(D) = \frac{1}{2}\mathbb{E}_{x\sim p_r}[(D(x) - 1)^2] + \frac{1}{2}\mathbb{E}_{z\sim p_z(z)}[(D(G(z)) + 1)^2]$$

$$\min_{G} L_{LSGAN}(G) = \frac{1}{2}\mathbb{E}_{z\sim p_r}[D(G(z))^2]$$

Another method for choosing a, b, and c parameters is to make G generate samples as realistically as possible by setting c = b. Using these values on the preceding equation, the loss becomes the following:

$$\min_{D} L_{LSGAN}(D) = \frac{1}{2}\mathbb{E}_{x \sim p_r}[(D(x) - 1)^2] + \frac{1}{2}\mathbb{E}_{z \sim p_z(z)}[D(G(z))^2]$$

$$\min_{G} L_{LSGAN}(G) = \frac{1}{2}\mathbb{E}_{z \sim p_r}[(D(G(z)) - 1)^2]$$

In Keras, the loss in the preceding equation is computed easily, as follows:

```
D_loss = 0.5 * (K.mean((D_real - 1)**2) + k.mean(D_fake**2))
G_loss = 0.5 * K.mean((D_fake - 1)**2)
```

The following screenshots are from scenes generated with LSGAN included in the *Least-Squares GAN* paper (`https://arxiv.org/abs/1611.04076`):

(a) Church outdoor.   (b) Dining room.

(c) Kitchen.   (d) Conference room.

Wasserstein GAN

The Wasserstein GAN (WGAN) framework, instead, uses the Wasserstein (Earth-Mover) distance between distributions, which in many cases does not suffer from loss explosion or vanishing gradient. In the WGAN framework, the loss functions of the generator and critic (which no longer emits a simple probability, but rather an approximation of the Wasserstein distance between the fake and real distributions) become the following:

$$\min_G L_{WGAN} = -\mathbb{E}_{\tilde{x} \sim P_g}[D(\tilde{x})]$$

$$\min_D L_{WGAN} = \mathbb{E}_{\tilde{x} \sim P_g} D(\tilde{x}) - \mathbb{E}_{x \sim P_r}[D(x)]$$

In this, P_r is the real distribution and P_g is the distribution learned by the generator. The original WGAN framework uses weight clipping to ensure that the critic satisfies a Lipschitz condition.

The following screenshots are from scenes in the *Wasserstein GAN* paper (`https://arxiv.org/abs/1701.07875`):

The implementation in Keras can be done with the following code. In the interest of just showing the needed parts, we remove plotting and other things that are not relevant here:

```
def scaled_mean(y, y_hat):
  return K.mean(y * y_hat)

def train(ndf=64, ngf=64, z_dim=100,
n_residual_blocks_discriminator=3,
  n_residual_blocks_generator=3, lr_d=1e-5, lr_g=1e-5,
  n_iterations=int(1e6), batch_size=128, n_checkpoint_images=36,
  out_dir='rgan_resnet'):
```

Get data shapes to instantiate models and build the models using the following code:

```
X_train, _ = get_data()
  image_shape = X_train[0].shape

  # build models
  input_shape_generator = (z_dim, )
  n_channels = image_shape[-1]
  input_shape_discriminator = image_shape

  D = build_cifar10_resnet_discriminator(
  input_shape_discriminator, ndf, n_residual_blocks_discriminator)
  G = build_cifar10_resnet_generator(
  input_shape_generator, ngf, n_residual_blocks_generator,
n_channels)
```

Define D graph, optimizer and scaled mean loss to compute 'expected' value of D(data):

```
D.compile(optimizer=RMSprop(lr_d), loss=scaled_mean)
```

Define D(G(z)) graph and optimizer:

```
D.trainable = False
  z = Input(shape=(z_dim, ))
  D_of_G = Model(inputs=z, outputs=D(G(z)))
```

Define Generator's Optimizer and scaled mean loss:

```
D_of_G.compile(RMSprop(lr=lr_g), loss=scaled_mean)
```

Define ones and minus ones to implement the Wasserstein GAN loss:

```
ones = np.ones((batch_size, 1), dtype=np.float32)
minus_ones = -ones
```

Instantiate variable to keep track of iterations iterations

```
gen_iters = 0
n_batches = int(len(X_train) / batch_size)
cur_batch = 0
```

Train the loop using the following code:

```
for i in range(n_iterations):
# follow the discriminator training schedule described in the
paper
if gen_iters < 25 or gen_iters % 500 == 0:
n_critic_iters = 100
else:
n_critic_iters = N_CRITIC_ITERS
```

Discriminator training loop and freeze generator weights is as follows:

```
D.trainable = True
G.trainable = False
for j in range(n_critic_iters):
# apply weight clipping as a proxy to achieve k-lipschitz
for l in D.layers:
weights = l.get_weights()
weights = [np.clip(w, -0.01, 0.01) for w in weights]
l.set_weights(weights)
```

Collect real and fake sample batch:

```
z = np.random.normal(0, 1, size=(batch_size, z_dim))
cur_ids = ids[cur_batch * batch_size:(cur_batch+1)*batch_size]
real_batch = X_train[cur_ids]
fake_batch = G.predict(z)
```

Compute discriminators loss, minus ones for real and ones for fake:

```
loss_real = D.train_on_batch(real_batch, minus_ones)
loss_fake = D.train_on_batch(fake_batch, ones)
cur_batch = (cur_batch + 1) % n_batches
```

Train the generator once, freeze discriminator weights and sample a new z vector:

```
D.trainable = False
 G.trainable = True
 z = np.random.normal(0, 1, size=(batch_size, z_dim))
 loss_g = D_of_G.train_on_batch(z, minus_ones)
 gen_iters += 1


train()
```

Wasserstein GAN with gradient penalty

Weight clipping can lead to problems with gradient stability. Instead, researchers suggests adding a gradient penalty to the critic's loss function, which indirectly tries to constrain the original critic's gradient to have a norm close to 1. Interestingly, in 2013, researchers proposed a method for directing neural networks to become k-Lipschitz by penalizing the objective function with the operator norm of the weights of each layer. The preceding equation thus becomes taken from the paper *Improved Training of Wassertein GANs* [59]) the following:

$$\min_{C} L_{WGAN-GP} = \mathbb{E}_{\tilde{x} \sim P_g} D(\tilde{x}) - \mathbb{E}_{x \sim P_r}[D(x)] + \lambda \mathbb{E}_{\hat{x} \sim P_{\hat{x}}}[(\|\nabla_{\hat{x}} D(\hat{x})\|_2 - 1)^2$$

The following screenshots are from scenes in the *Improved Training of Wasserstein GANs* paper (https://arxiv.org/abs/1704.00028):

In Keras and TensorFlow, the Wasserstein GAN with gradient Penalty can be implemented with a few modifications the code we had before. First let's implement a few auxiliary functions.

The `loss_gradient_penalty` methods will be used for computing the gradient penalty loss. Since we can only pass two arguments directly to loss functions in Keras, `y_true` and `y_pred`, we will have to take advantage of the `partial()` method to link the `averaged_samples` to a symbolic variable and the `gradient_penalty_weight` to a global constant. Our implementation is based of the `keras-contrib implementation` and in the interest of just showing the needed parts, we remove plotting and other things that are not relevant here.

```
def loss_gradient_penalty(y_true, y_pred, averaged_samples,
gradient_penalty_weight):
    # compute the gradients of the discriminator outputs with respect to
the averaged_samples
    gradients = K.gradients(y_pred, averaged_samples)[0]
    # compute the euclidean norm of the gradient by squaring ...
    gradients_sqr = K.square(gradients)
    # ... then summing over the rows ...
    gradients_sqr_sum = K.sum(gradients_sqr, axis=np.arange(1,
len(gradients_sqr.shape)))
    # ... and taking the square root
    gradient_l2_norm = K.sqrt(gradients_sqr_sum)
    # compute lambda * (gradient_l2_norm - 1)^2
    gradient_penalty = gradient_penalty_weight * K.square(gradient_l2_norm
- 1)
    # return the mean value
    return K.mean(gradient_penalty)
```

Conversely, computing the l2 norm in the function above can be written in a more succinct way, leading to the following implementation:

```
def loss_gradient_penalty(y_true, y_pred, averaged_samples,
gradient_penalty_weight):
    # compute the gradients of the discriminator outputs with respect to
the averaged_samples
    gradients = K.gradients(y_pred, averaged_samples)[0]

    # compute the l2 norm of the gradients
    gradient_l2_norm = K.sqrt(K.sum(K.batch_flatten(K.square(gradients)),
axis=1, keepdims=True))

    # compute lambda * (gradient_l2_norm - 1)^2
    gradient_penalty = gradient_penalty_weight * K.square(gradient_l2_norm
- 1)
```

```
# return the mean value
return K.mean(gradient_penalty)
```

We also need a function to compute the random weighted average between real samples and fake samples.

```
class RandomWeightedAverage(_Merge):
    def _merge_function(self, inputs):
        # uniformly sample the number line between 0 and 1
        weights = K.random_uniform((BATCH_SIZE, 1, 1, 1))

        # return the weighted average
        return inputs[0] + (inputs[1] - inputs[0]) * weights
```

Now that the auxiliary functions have been implemented, let's implement the Wasserstein GAN with gradient penalty the following way:

```
def scaled_mean(y, y_hat):
    return K.mean(y * y_hat)

def train(ndf=128, ngf=128, z_dim=128,
n_residual_blocks_discriminator=3,
            n_residual_blocks_generator=3, lr_d=2e-4, lr_g=2e-4,
            n_iterations=int(1e6), batch_size=128,
n_checkpoint_images=36,
            out_dir='wgan-gp_resnet_nobn'):
```

Set BATCH_SIZE to be global using the following code:

```
global BATCH_SIZE
    BATCH_SIZE = batch_size
```

Get data shapes to instantiate models:

```
X_train, _ = get_data()
    image_shape = X_train[0].shape
```

Build models using the following code:

```
input_shape_generator = (z_dim, )
    n_channels = image_shape[-1]
    input_shape_discriminator = image_shape

    D = build_cifar10_resnet_discriminator(
        input_shape_discriminator, ndf,
n_residual_blocks_discriminator)
    G = build_cifar10_resnet_generator(
```

```
            input_shape_generator, ngf, n_residual_blocks_generator,
    n_channels)
```

Instantiate variables to use when compiling model graphs:

```
real_samples = Input(shape=X_train.shape[1:])
    z = Input(shape=(z_dim, ))
    fake_samples = G(z)
    averaged_samples = RandomWeightedAverage()([real_samples,
    fake_samples])
```

Define D outputs to compute losses:

```
D_real = D(real_samples)
    D_fake = D(fake_samples)
    D_averaged = D(averaged_samples)
```

Use partial to set `averaged_samples` to the symbolic tensor:

```
loss_gp = partial(loss_gradient_penalty,
                    averaged_samples=averaged_samples,
    gradient_penalty_weight=GRADIENT_PENALTY_WEIGHT)
    loss_gp.__name__ = 'loss_gradient_penalty'
```

Define D graph and optimizer:

```
G.trainable = False
    D.trainable = True
    D_model = Model(inputs=[real_samples, z],
                    outputs=[D_real, D_fake, D_averaged])
    # we use scaled mean for D_real and D_fake and loss_gp for
    D_averaged
    D_model.compile(optimizer=Adam(lr_d, beta_1=0.5, beta_2=0.9),
                    loss=[scaled_mean, scaled_mean, loss_gp])
```

Define D(G(z)) graph for training the Generator:

```
G.trainable = True
    D.trainable = False
    G_model = Model(inputs=z, outputs=D_fake)
```

Define Generator's Optimizer:

```
G_model.compile(Adam(lr=lr_g, beta_1=0.5, beta_2=0.9),
                loss=scaled_mean)
```

Define `ones`, `minus_ones` and `dummy` to implement the Wasserstein GAN loss with GP:

```
ones = np.ones((batch_size, 1), dtype=np.float32)
    minus_ones = -ones
    dummy = np.zeros((batch_size, 1), dtype=np.float32)
```

Instantiate variable to keep track of iterations iterations:

```
gen_iters = 0
    n_batches = int(len(X_train) / batch_size)
    cur_batch = 0
    epoch = 0
```

The training loop is as follows:

```
for i in range(n_iterations):
        # discriminator training loop, freeze generator weights
        D.trainable = True
        G.trainable = False

        for j in range(N_CRITIC_ITERS):
            # collect real and fake sample batch
            z = np.random.normal(0, 1, size=(batch_size, z_dim))
            cur_ids = ids[cur_batch *
batch_size:(cur_batch+1)*batch_size]
            real_batch = X_train[cur_ids]
```

Compute discriminators loss, minus ones for real and ones for fake, dummy for GP:

```
loss_real, loss_fake, loss_gp, _ = D_model.train_on_batch(
                [real_batch, z],
                [minus_ones, ones, dummy])
        cur_batch = (cur_batch + 1) % n_batches
```

Train the generator once, freeze discriminator weights and sample a new z vector:

```
D.trainable = False
        G.trainable = True
        z = np.random.normal(0, 1, size=(batch_size, z_dim))
        loss_g = G_model.train_on_batch(z, minus_ones)
        gen_iters += 1
        cur_batch = (cur_batch + 1) % n_batches

    train()
```

Relativistic GAN

In a ground-breaking paper *The relativistic discriminator: a key element missing from standard GAN* by Alexia Jolicoeur-Martineau, it is argued that standard GAN, as described in Ian Goodfellow's first paper, is missing a fundamental property: training the generator should not only increase the probability that fake data is real, but also decrease the probability that real data is real.

Relativistic GANs are not completely new, as the Wasserstein GAN, the Wasserstein GAP with Gradient Penalty and the Least- Squares GAN already have a relativistic discriminator. These approaches are classified asThis possibly explains why these approaches are more standard GANs. Fortunately, the standard GANs can also be modified to become relativistic.

Giving this property to the discriminator makes the standard GAN relativistic. As we will show, the discriminator of any GAN loss can be made to be relativistic. Interestingly, IPM-based GANs (WGAN, WGAN-GP, and so on) already have a relativistic discriminator. This explains in part why such approaches are generally much more stable than standard GAN; relativism improves image quality and training stability.

As it is described in Alexia's paper, GANs like the Wasserstein GAN and the Least-Squares GAN are based on Integral Probability Metrics(IPMS). IPMs are a class of divergences such that:

$$IPM_F(\mathbb{P} \parallel \mathbb{Q}) = \sup_{C \in \mathcal{F}} \mathbb{E}_{x \sim \mathbb{P}}[C(x)] - \mathbb{E}_{x \sim \mathbb{Q}}[C(x)],$$

where $\mathcal{F}$ is a class of real-valued functions, sup is the supremum, and the divergence between distributions $\mathbb{P}$ and $\mathbb{Q}$ is computed as the supremum over the distance between the expected values of $C(x)$ computed over $x \sim \mathbb{P}$ and $x \sim \mathbb{Q}$. The attentive reader will note that this distance metric is directly related to the Wasserstein distance described earlier in this chapter.

Let's now take a look at the discriminator's loss function defined in the standard GAN (SGAN) paper:

$$D(x) = sigmoid(C(x)),$$

where in this formula $C(x)$ represents the outputs of the Discriminator before the non-linearity on the last layer.

Note that in this definition of the objective function, there's no explicit interaction between the discriminator's output on real data and fake data. In this form, a discriminator will continue to optimize its loss on real data even though an equilibrium between the discriminator and generator has already been reached.

In her paper, Alexia proposes the Relativistic Standard GAN (RSGAN) loss for the discriminator as the following:

$$D(\tilde{x}) = sigmoid(C(x_r) - C(x_f)),$$

Here, x_r and x_f represent samples from real and fake distributions, $\tilde{x} = (x_r, x_f) \sim (\mathbb{P}, \mathbb{Q})$, while C represents the output of a discriminator, here called *Critic*, taking inspiration from Martin Arjovski's Wasserstein GAN paper. Note that in this definition there is an explicit interaction between the discriminator's output on real and fake data. As a matter of fact, the loss represents the odd ratio.

Alexia further develops RSGAN with the Relativistic Average SGAN (RASGAN), where the loss function is now the following:

$$D(x) = \begin{cases} sigmoid(C(x) - \mathbb{E}_{x_f \sim \mathbb{P}} C(x_r)), & \text{if } x \text{ is real} \\ sigmoid(C(x) - \mathbb{E}_{x_r \sim \mathbb{P}} C(x_r)), & \text{if } x \text{ is fake} \end{cases}$$

In our repository we provide an implementation that uses the Relativistic GAN. The following image grid has images generated by a Generator trained using the Relativistic GAN loss:

Fake Cats. Copied from the paper *The relativistic discriminator: a key element missing from standard GAN* (https://arxiv.org/abs/1807.00734)

Summary

In this chapter, we learned about the challenges faced while training GANs and how to address them. We also learned some tips and tricks that we can utilize while training GANs. We then looked at various GAN model architectures and what they are used for. Finally, we learned about a number of algorithms used in GANs, along with their implementation details.

In the next chapter, we will look at how to synthesize images using GANs.

3
Section 3: Application of GANs in Computer Vision, Natural Language Processing, and Audio

In section three, you will implement state-of-the-art models for computer vision, natural language processing, and audio processing using GANs.

The following chapters will be covered in this section:

- Chapter 6, *pix2pixHD – Synthesizing and Manipulating Images with GANs*
- Chapter 7, *Progressive Growing of GANs*
- Chapter 8, *Generation of Discrete Sequences Using GANs*
- Chapter 9, *Text-To-Image Synthesis with GANs*
- Chapter 10, *Speech Enhancement with GANs*
- Chapter 11, *TequilaGAN: Identifying GAN Samples*
- Chapter 12, *What's Next in GANs*

6
Synthesizing and Manipulating Images with GANs

In this chapter, you will learn how to implement a model based on pix2pixHD, a method for high-resolution (for example, 2048x1024), photo-realistic image-to-image translation. pix2pixHD can be used for many exciting tasks, such as turning semantic label maps into photo-realistic images, or synthesizing portraits from face label maps.

After a brief introduction to the topic of image-to-image translation, we are going to implement a baseline model using the pix2pix setup and train it on the Zappos dataset, which contains images of shoes on a white background and their respective outlines.

After implementing the pix2pix baseline, we will implement a model based on pix2pixHD and train it on the Cityscapes dataset, which focuses on the semantic understanding of urban street scenes and includes images of such scenes and their respective semantic label maps.

The following topics will be covered in this chapter:

- Image-to-image translation
- Experimental setup
- pix2pix implementation
- pix2pixHD implementation

Technical requirements

In this chapter, we will focus on the UT Zappos 50K dataset, which can be downloaded from `http://vision.cs.utexas.edu/projects/finegrained/utzap50k/`, and the Cityscapes dataset, which can be downloaded from `https://www.cityscapes-dataset.com/`.

We will rely on the software libraries included in our Docker container, available at `https://github.com/packt/hands_on_gans_with_keras/blob/master/Dockerfile`.

You can visit the GitHub repo of this book for the full code files at `https://github.com/PacktPublishing/Hands-On-Generative-Adversarial-Networks-with-Keras`.

Image-to-image translation

Despite the language-based name, image-to-image translation consists of synthesizing an image based on another image. This is also known as conditional image synthesis. A well-known example of conditional image synthesis is image colorization, which involves converting a black and white image into a color image.

Image-to-image translation is a complex task, because a single source image can have multiple possible translations, thus requiring a model and a loss function that are able to choose between these possible translations instead of picking one.

For example, consider a non-autoregressive model trained to colorize black and white images by minimizing the L2 or L1 image reconstruction loss. This model will have several issues because, when conditioned on the source black and white image, it will learn to predict the mean or median image from all possible colorizations from the source image.

Using the GAN framework for image-to-image translation is attractive for multiple reasons: first, the Generator is able to sample from the underlying distribution of the latent vector and use it as an extra condition to disambiguate between possible solutions; second, the GAN framework does not require hand-engineering features that represent characteristics in the images that we are interested in; and lastly, the GAN framework is not required to define a loss that describes the image-to-image translation characteristics we want to learn.

Conditional image synthesis with GANs has been applied successfully to multiple tasks, including synthesizing photos from label maps, reconstructing objects from edge maps, and converting black and white images to color images, to name just a few.

Experimental setup

In this chapter, we are going to investigate image-to-image translation by using the pix2pix and pix2pixHD models. We are going to synthesize shoes from shoe outlines and synthesize urban Cityscapes from instance and semantic maps. We will start with the simplest model: pix2pix.

Data

The dataset we are going to use consists of 50,000 training images from the UT Zappos 50K dataset, also known as UT-Zap50K. The dataset consists of approximately 50,000 catalog images collected from Zappos.com (https://www.zappos.com) and their respective edge maps. All images are centered on a white background and pictured in the same orientation. It contains four types of footwear, including shoes, sandals, slippers, and boots. This is the data we are going to use to train pix2pix.

In the improved implementation (pix2pixHD), we will use the Cityscapes dataset. The Cityscapes dataset consists of semantic, instance-wise, dense pixel annotations of 30 classes, including cars, trees, and pedestrians, to name just a few. It has 5,000 images with high-quality annotations and 20,000 images with coarse annotations.

Let's take a look at the following steps regarding helper functions, which we will use to load the data and iterate over minibatches when training pix2pix:

1. We begin by importing the various libraries:

```
import numpy as np
from glob import glob
from PIL import Image
```

2. Define a simple function to load and scale images to [-1, 1]:

```
def load_image(filepath):
    images = np.array(Image.open(filepath), dtype=int)
    images = 2 * (images / 255.0) - 1
    images = images.astype(float)
    return images
```

3. Define a function to iterate over minibatches:

```
def iterate_minibatches(glob_str, batch_size=128, img_size=256):
    # get a list of all filepaths based on the glob str
    filepaths = glob(glob_str)
    n_files = len(filepaths)
    cur_batch = 0
```

4. Wrap the iteration in a `while` loop to serve batches forever:

```
while True:
        # drop last if it does not fit
        if (n_files - cur_batch*batch_size) < batch_size or
cur_batch == 0:
            ids = np.random.randint(0, n_files, n_files)
            np.random.shuffle(ids)
            cur_batch = 0
```

5. Create an array to store image pairs (images, edges):

```
train_data = []
        for i in range(batch_size):
            image_ab =
load_image(filepaths[ids[cur_batch*batch_size+i]])
            train_data.append([image_ab[:, :img_size], image_ab[:,
img_size:]])
```

6. Increment the batch count and `yield` the data:

```
cur_batch = (cur_batch + 1) % int(len(filepaths)/batch_size)
        train_data = np.array(train_data)
        yield train_data, cur_batch
```

Training

In this subsection, we will look at the parts required to train the Discriminator and the Generator. We will look at library and function imports; the training function, including its signature; variable setup and body; and logging functions. Let's start with the imports, as usual.

Imports

The imports we are going to use in pix2pix are very similar to the imports we will use in other chapters of the book. Here, we take advantage of `tensorboardX` to easily visualize the training progress and many other things:

```
import numpy as np
from keras.models import Model
from keras.layers import Input
from keras.optimizers import Adam
from models import build_discriminator, build_generator
from tensorboardX import SummaryWriter
from data_utils import iterate_minibatches, log_images, log_losses
```

Our implementation of pix2pix does not use any global variables, so we can directly look at the `train` method itself.

Training signature

The `train` method signature used for pix2pix is similar to other train signatures that we use in this book. Let's take a look at the following training method signature:

```
def train(data_folderpath='data/edges2shoes', image_size=256,
ndf=64,
        ngf=64, lr_d=2e-4, lr_g=2e-4, n_iterations=int(1e6),
        batch_size=64, iters_per_checkpoint=100,
n_checkpoint_samples=16,
        out_dir='gan'):
```

Th following is a table describing each argument:

Argument	Description
data_folderpath	Folderpath to the dataset.
image_size	Image height or width. Assumes square image.
ndf, ngf	Number of Discriminator and Generator filters base.
lr_d, lr_g	Learning rate of the Discriminator and Generator.
n_iterations, batch_size, iters_per_checkpoint	Self-descriptive.
n_checkpoint_samples	Number of samples to log on each checkpoint.
out_dir	Path to directory where outputs will be saved.

The attentive reader will notice that this set of arguments is not specific to training GANs, but is general to routines in which the parameters of a model are estimated iteratively. Let's now look at the training setup.

Training setup

The training setup for pix2pix is similar to the training setup we had to train our first GAN. Here, we have added a few nice features, including logging losses and images, computing patch sizes to initialize variables that are used in computing the loss and other things. The following are the various steps involved in training the Discriminator and the Generator:

1. Instantiate the loggers:

```
logger = SummaryWriter(out_dir)
logger.add_scalar('d_lr', lr_d, 0)
logger.add_scalar('g_lr', lr_g, 0)
```

2. Instantiate a data iterator for `train` and validation:

```
data_iterator = iterate_minibatches(
    data_folderpath + "/train/*.jpg", batch_size, image_size)
val_data_iterator = iterate_minibatches(
    data_folderpath + "/val/*.jpg", n_checkpoint_samples,
image_size)
```

3. Instantiate fixed images for evaluation:

```
img_ab_fixed, _ = next(val_data_iterator)
img_a_fixed, img_b_fixed = img_ab_fixed[:, 0], img_ab_fixed[:, 1]
img_a_shape = img_a_fixed.shape[1:]
img_b_shape = img_b_fixed.shape[1:]
```

4. Add the `patch` size to use with variables for computing losses:

```
patch = int(img_a_shape[0] / 2**4) # n_layers
disc_patch = (patch, patch, 1)
print("img a shape ", img_a_shape)
print("img b shape ", img_b_shape)
print("disc_patch ", disc_patch)
```

5. Plot real text for reference:

```
log_images(img_a_fixed, 'real_a', '0', logger)
log_images(img_b_fixed, 'real_b', '0', logger)
```

6. Build the `D` and `G` models:

```
D = build_discriminator(
    img_a_shape, img_b_shape, ndf, activation='sigmoid')
G = build_generator(img_a_shape, ngf)
```

7. Build the model outputs: `img_a` is edge and `img_b` is image:

```
img_a_input = Input(shape=img_a_shape)
img_b_input = Input(shape=img_b_shape)
fake_samples = G(img_a_input)
D_real = D([img_a_input, img_b_input])
D_fake = D([img_a_input, fake_samples])
```

8. Include image reconstruction loss for the Generator:

```
loss_reconstruction = partial(mean_absolute_error,
 real_samples=img_b_input,
 fake_samples=fake_samples)
loss_reconstruction.__name__ = 'loss_reconstruction'
```

9. Define the `D` graph and `optimizer`:

```
G.trainable = False
D.trainable = True
D_model = Model(inputs=[img_a_input, img_b_input],
                outputs=[D_real, D_fake])
D_model.compile(optimizer=Adam(lr_d, beta_1=0.5, beta_2=0.9),
                loss='binary_crossentropy')
```

10. Define the $D(G(z))$ graph and optimizer, and return `fake_samples` to compute reconstruction loss:

```
G.trainable = True
D.trainable = False
G_model = Model(inputs=[img_a_input, img_b_input],
                outputs=[D_fake, fake_samples])
G_model.compile(Adam(lr=lr_g, beta_1=0.5, beta_2=0.999),
                loss=['binary_crossentropy', loss_reconstruction],
                loss_weights=[1, reconstruction_weight])
```

11. Instantiate variables for computing losses:

```
ones = np.ones((batch_size, ) + disc_patch, dtype=np.float32)
zeros = np.zeros((batch_size, ) + disc_patch, dtype=np.float32)
dummy = zeros
```

In summary, we set up the loggers, the data loaders, the models, and their respective loss functions. Now, let's look at the training loop.

Training loop

With the exception of the reconstruction loss between fake and real images, the following pix2pix training loop is rather straightforward and is similar to the first GAN we implemented in this book:

```
for i in range(n_iterations):
    # only D weights are trainable
    D.trainable = True
    G.trainable = False
    # sample data and train D using GAN loss
    image_ab_batch, _ = next(data_iterator)
    loss_d = D_model.train_on_batch(
        [image_ab_batch[:, 0], image_ab_batch[:, 1]],
        [ones, zeros])

    # only G weight are trainable
    D.trainable = False
    G.trainable = True

    # sample data and train using GAN loss and reconstruction loss
    image_ab_batch, _ = next(data_iterator)
    loss_g = G_model.train_on_batch(
        [image_ab_batch[:, 0], image_ab_batch[:, 1]],
        [ones, dummy])

    # report losses and eventually plot images
    print("iter", i)
    if (i % iters_per_checkpoint) == 0:
        G.trainable = False
        fake_image = G.predict(img_a_fixed)
        log_images(fake_image, 'val_fake', i, logger)
    log_losses(loss_d, loss_g, i, logger)

train()
```

Before diving into the model implementation, let's implement two logging functions that facilitate the evaluation of the training process.

Logging

In pix2pix, we are going to use logging functions: one for logging images and another for logging losses.

The first one, `log_images`, leverages tensorboardX's `add_image` method to add images to a Tensorboard log. The method takes as input a tag, an image, and an index number associated with this addition to the log, height, and channel format to be used:

```
def log_images(images, name, i, logger, n_rows, n_cols, n_channels,
shape=4):
    # get shape to create a square image grid
    dim = int(np.sqrt(images.shape))
    # create an image grid
    images = (images.reshape(dim, dim, n_rows, n_cols, n_channels)
                 .transpose(0, 2, 1, 3, 4)
                 .reshape(4*n_rows, 4*n_cols, n_channels))
    # scale back to [0, 1]
    images = ((images + 1) * 0.5)
    # add image to tensorboard log
    logger.add_image('{}'.format(name, i), images, i, dataformats='HWC')
```

The second one, `log_losses`, leverages tensorboardX's `add_scaler` to add plots to a Tensorboard log. The method takes as input a tag, a scalar value, and an index number associated with this addition to the log:

```
def log_losses(loss_d, loss_g, iteration, logger):
    logger.add_scalar("loss_d", loss_d[0], iteration)
    logger.add_scalar("loss_d_real", loss_d[1], iteration)
    logger.add_scalar("loss_d_fake", loss_d[2], iteration)
    logger.add_scalar("loss_g", loss_g, iteration)
```

Now that we have most of the experimental setup done, let's implement the Discriminator and Generator.

pix2pix implementation

pix2pix implementation has two interesting novelties with respect to the previous chapters, including a PatchGAN Discriminator and the U-Net architecture. Unlike other Discriminator architectures, the PatchGAN Discriminator outputs multiple values per image. The U-Net architecture is used on the Generator and includes a skip connection between layers of the Generator that are increasingly far from each other.

The layers used in pix2pix models can be summarized in two blocks: one block is the encoding block, which is a stack of a convolution with batch normalization and a leaky ReLU non-linearity; the other block is the decoding block, which is a stack of upsampled convolutions with batch normalization and ReLU non-linearity. The decoding block has a skip connection that concatenates a skip input to the layers' output.

The imports used in modeling pix2pix do not offer us any novelty. Let's skip them this time and look at the custom layers that are designed to make the code more readable.

Custom layers

In the pix2pix implementation, there are many code blocks that are repeated. So, we wrap such blocks into individual methods for ease of use. As we described earlier, we will need an encoding block and a decoding block. The novelty is in the skip input in the decoding block that concatenates the layer output with the layer input:

```
def encoding_block(x, n_filters, kernel_size=4, strides=2):
    x = Conv2D(n_filters, kernel_size=kernel_size, strides=strides,
               padding='same')(x)
    x = BatchNormalization(momentum=0.8)(x)
    x = LeakyReLU(alpha=0.2)(x)
    return x

def decoding_block(x, skip_input, n_filters, kernel_size=4):
    x = UpSampling2D(size=2)(x)
    x = Conv2D(n_filters, kernel_size=kernel_size, strides=1,
padding='same')(x)
    x = BatchNormalization()(x)
    x = Activation('relu')(x)
    x = Dropout(0.5)(x)
    x = Concatenate()([x, skip_input])
    return x
```

Discriminator

The Discriminator used in pix2pix is called **PatchGAN**. Unlike other Discriminators that output a single value per image, the PatchGAN Discriminator outputs multiple values per image, where each value corresponds to a patch on the image. This can be achieved by stacking convolutions until the desired number of patches is reached. Once the number of patches is reached, you project the output of that convolution to a single channel to obtain a single value per patch. This single value per patch represents the output of the Discriminator with respect to that patch:

```
def build_discriminator(input_shape_a=(256, 256, 3), input_shape_b=(256,
    256, 3),
                        ndf=64, n_layers=3, kernel_size=4, strides=2,
                        activation='linear'):
    """PatchGAN discriminator"""
    # inputs are source and target images
```

```
input_a = Input(shape=input_shape_a)
input_b = Input(shape=input_shape_b)
x = Concatenate(axis=-1)([input_a, input_b])

# convolutional front-end
x = Conv2D(ndf, kernel_size=kernel_size, strides=2, padding='same')(x)
x = LeakyReLU(alpha=0.2)(x)

# create encoding blocks
for i in range(1, n_layers):
    x = encoding_block(x, ndf * (2**i), kernel_size)

# convolutional back-end
ndf_mult = min(2 ** n_layers, 8)
x = Conv2D(ndf * ndf_mult, kernel_size=kernel_size, strides=strides,
padding='same')(x)
x = LeakyReLU(alpha=0.2)(x)
x = BatchNormalization()(x)

# project to a single channel
x = Conv2D(1, kernel_size=kernel_size, strides=1, padding='same')(x)
x = Activation(activation)(x)

# create model graph
model = Model(inputs=[input_a, input_b], outputs=x,
name='Discriminator')
print("\nDiscriminator")
model.summary()
return model
```

Generator

The Generator used in pix2pix is a U-Net Generator, which consists of a stack of encoding blocks followed by a stack of decoding blocks. Each encoding block is connected to a decoding block by skip connections between them, via concatenation. In the U-Net architecture, skip connections are created by going through encoding layers from first to last and adding a skip connection between that layer and the farthest decoding layer that does not have a connection. The U-Net name comes from the fact that the distance between layers diminishes as we move through the encoding layers, resembling a U-shape.

This architecture is similar to the architecture we will implement in the **SEGAN (Sound Enhancement GAN)** chapter:

```python
def build_generator(input_shape=(256, 256, 3), ngf=64, kernel_size=4,
strides=2):
    """U-Net Generator"""
    image_input = Input(shape=input_shape)
    n_channels = input_shape[-1]

    # encoding blocks
    e1 = Conv2D(ngf, kernel_size=kernel_size, strides=2,
padding='same')(image_input)
    e1 = LeakyReLU(alpha=0.2)(e1)
    e2 = encoding_block(e1, ngf*2)
    e3 = encoding_block(e2, ngf*4)
    e4 = encoding_block(e3, ngf*8)
    e5 = encoding_block(e4, ngf*8)
    e6 = encoding_block(e5, ngf*8)
    x = encoding_block(e6, ngf*8)

    # decoding blocks
    x = decoding_block(x, e6, ngf*8)
    x = decoding_block(x, e5, ngf*8)
    x = decoding_block(x, e4, ngf*8)
    x = decoding_block(x, e3, ngf*4)
    x = decoding_block(x, e2, ngf*2)
    x = decoding_block(x, e1, ngf)

    x = UpSampling2D(size=2)(x)
    x = Conv2D(n_channels, kernel_size=4, strides=1, padding='same')(x)
    x = Activation('tanh')(x)

    # create model graph
    model = Model(inputs=image_input, outputs=x, name='Generator')
    print("\nGenerator")
    model.summary()
    return model
```

Now that we have covered the full experimental setup, we can start training our own model. In the following image, we provide a grid of images produced with a Generator trained for 10,000 iterations of our code on the Zappos shoes dataset:

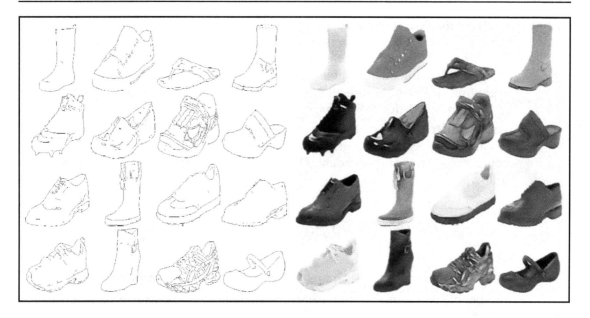

Note that the edge maps have a strong influence on the images produced by the Generator, as can be confirmed, for example, by the red shoe, whose respective edge map does not have edges for laces either.

pix2pixHD implementation

As the name suggests, pix2pixHD is a high-definition improvement on the pix2pix baseline. Let's take a look at some of the improvements on pix2pix. It was developed by Ting-Chun Wang et al. and published in the paper *High-Resolution Image Synthesis and Semantic Manipulation with Conditional GANs*. In this subsection, we are going to gain an understanding of, and implement, some of the improvements to pix2pix that were proposed in the pix2pixHD paper.

Improvements to pix2pix

The following are the improvements made in pix2pixHD compared with pix2pix:

- **Coarse-to-fine Generator**: Multiple Generators are used and each of them produce an image that will be subsumed by the next Generator that produces an image at a higher resolution. Practically speaking, though, pix2pixHD only uses two Generators.

- **Multi-scale Discriminators**: Multiple Discriminators are used and each of them operates on a subsampled version of the image. With such a setup, in which the Discriminator operating on the lower resolution has a global view of the full image but less information about fine details, the Discriminator operating on the higher resolution has more attention to fine details but less information about the global characteristics of the image.
- **Feature matching loss**: Feature matching loss minimizes the mean absolute distance between the outputs from different layers of the Discriminator computed on real and fake data. The feature matching loss is calculated as follows:

$$L_{FM}(G, D_k) = \mathbb{E}_{(s,x)} \sum_{i=1}^{T} \frac{1}{N_i} [|| \ D_k^{(i)}(s, x) - D_k^{(i)}(s, G(s))||_1]$$

Here, s represents semantic maps, x represents images, T represents the total number of layers, and N_i represents the number of elements in each layer.

- **Instance edges**: The Pix2pixHD authors argue that the most important information provided by instance maps are the boundaries, or edges, between object instances. This is especially true when instance maps are combined with semantic maps, because, while semantic maps provide the same labels for objects in the same class, instance maps complement semantic maps by providing the boundaries between these objects:

Left: Semantic label map. Right: Instance map and boundaries

We are going to improve our pix2pix baseline by adding **multi-scale Discriminators, feature matching loss**, and **Instance edges**.

The imports used in modeling pix2pixHD do not offer us any novelty. Let's skip them again and look at the custom layers that are designed to make the code more readable.

Custom layers

To facilitate building the networks used in pix2pixHD, we create a `resnet_block` function. The function is very similar to ResNet blocks we have built in other chapters of this book. The reflection padding method used in this code has been added to our GitHub repository and was made available on Stack Overflow by the user jeevaa_v:

```
def resnet_block(input, n_filters):
    x = input
    x = ReflectionPadding2D(padding=1)(x)
    x = Conv2D(n_filters, kernel_size=3, strides=1, padding='valid')(x)
    x = BatchNormalization()(x)
    x = Activation('relu')(x)
    x = ReflectionPadding2D(padding=1)(x)
    x = Conv2D(n_filters, kernel_size=3, strides=1, padding='valid')(x)
    x = BatchNormalization()(x)

    # Residual Connection
    x = Add()([input, x])
    return x
```

Now that we have defined the custom layer, let's use it to implement the Discriminator and the Generator.

Discriminator

As we described earlier, the Discriminator architecture used in pix2pixHD is similar to pix2pix. The main difference between them is the number of Discriminators and the fact that, in pix2pixHD, the Discriminators look at images at different resolutions. The Discriminator has an argument that specifies how many times the input data will be downsampled. This is used to obtain multi-scale Discriminators that operate on coarse and fine resolutions.

Another important difference in the Discriminator used in pix2pixHD is the intermediate layer outputs that will be used in the feature matching loss:

```
def build_discriminator(input_shape_a=(2048, 1024, 1),
                        input_shape_b=(2048, 1024, 3),
                        input_shape_c=(2048, 1024, 1),
                        ndf=64, n_layers=3,
                        kernel_size=4, strides=2, activation='linear',
                        n_downsampling=1, name='Discriminator'):
```

Declare inputs for the semantic map, image, and edges map:

```
input_a = Input(shape=input_shape_a)
    input_b = Input(shape=input_shape_b)
    input_c = Input(shape=input_shape_c)
```

Create a placeholder for collecting intermediate layer outputs:

```
features = []
```

Downsample the data as follows:

```
x = Concatenate(axis=-1)([input_a, input_b, input_c])
    for i in range(n_downsampling):
        x = AveragePooling2D(3, strides=2, padding='same')(x)
        x = Conv2D(ndf, kernel_size=kernel_size, strides=2,
padding='same')(x)
        x = LeakyReLU(alpha=0.2)(x)
        features.append(x)
```

Create a stack of convolutions with `BatchNormalization` and `LeakyReLU`:

```
nf = ndf
    for i in range(1, n_layers):
        nf = min(ndf * 2, 512)
        x = Conv2D(nf, kernel_size=kernel_size, strides=2,
padding='same')(x)
        x = BatchNormalization()(x)
        x = LeakyReLU(alpha=0.2)(x)
        features.append(x)
```

The following is the code and another ConvBatchNormLeakyrelu with `strides=1`:

```
nf = min(nf * 2, 512)
    x = Conv2D(nf, kernel_size=kernel_size, strides=1, padding='same')(x)
    x = BatchNormalization()(x)
    x = LeakyReLU(alpha=0.2)(x)
    features.append(x)
```

The following is the code and project for multiple patches, patchGAN:

```
x = Conv2D(1, kernel_size=kernel_size, strides=1, padding='same')(x)
    x = Activation(activation)(x)
```

Create the model graph and the outputs intermediate features as well:

```
model = Model(inputs=[input_a, input_b, input_c], outputs=[x] + features,
name=name)
    print("\nDiscriminator")
    model.summary()
    return model
```

Now, let's take a look at the Generator.

Generator

In pix2pixHD, we start with the Generator, call it the global Generator, which operates on images that have a lower resolution than the target resolution. After the global Generator is trained, another Generator, call it the local enhancer, is appended to the global Generator and both networks are trained jointly. The global Generator produces images that will be subsumed by the local enhancer to produce images with a higher resolution than the global Generator:

```
def build_global_generator(segmap_shape=(2048, 1024, 1),
                           edges_shape=(2048, 1024, 1),
                           ngf=64, n_downsampling=3, n_resnet_blocks=9,
                           n_channels=3):
    segmaps = Input(shape=segmap_shape)
    edges = Input(shape=edges_shape)
    inputs = Concatenate(axis=-1)([segmaps, edges])

    # front end
    x = ReflectionPadding2D(3)(inputs)
    x = Conv2D(ngf, kernel_size=7, strides=1, padding='valid')(x)
    x = BatchNormalization()(x)
    x = Activation('relu')(x)

    # downsample
    for i in range(n_downsampling):
        mult = 2**i
        x = Conv2D(ngf * mult * 2, kernel_size=3, strides=2,
padding='same')(x)
        x = BatchNormalization()(x)
        x = Activation('relu')(x)
    # residual blocks
    mult = 2**n_downsampling
    for i in range(n_resnet_blocks):
        x = resnet_block(x, ngf*mult)
    # upsample
    for i in range(n_downsampling):
```

```
        mult = 2**(n_downsampling - i)
    x = Conv2DTranspose(filters=int(ngf * mult / 2), kernel_size=3,
                        strides=2, padding='same')(x)
    x = BatchNormalization()(x)
    x = Activation('relu')(x)

    # residual connection for local generator
    residual = x

    # final convolution
    x = ReflectionPadding2D(3)(x)
    x = Conv2D(n_channels, kernel_size=7, strides=1, padding='valid')(x)
    x = Activation('tanh')(x)

    # create model graph, output residual for coarse generators
    model = Model(inputs=[segmaps, edges], outputs=[x, residual],
                  name='GlobalGenerator')

    print("\nGlobal Generator")
    model.summary()
    return model
```

Although we will only implement the global Generator in this chapter, in our GitHub repository, we provide the building blocks for coupling the global Generator with the local enhancer, and invite readers to implement it as an exercise.

Now that we have improved the Generator and the Discriminator, we need to make modifications to our experimental setup.

Training

The training loop for pix2pixHD is certainly more complex than pix2pix, given the feature matching loss, the number of inputs, and many other things. Let's start with the helper functions.

Helper functions

In pix2pixHD, we use the intermediate outputs of the Discriminator to compute the feature matching loss. The implementation is straightforward: we first collect the intermediate layer outputs from the Discriminator on real and fake samples, and then we compute the mean absolute distance between these intermediate outputs:

```
def loss_feature_matching(y_true, fake_samples, lbl_map, real_samples,
                          edges_map, D, feature_matching_weight=10):

    # get the discriminator intermediate outputs from fake and real data
    f_fake = D([lbl_map, fake_samples, edges_map])[1:]
    f_real = D([lbl_map, real_samples, edges_map])[1:]
    loss_feat_match = 0

    # sum the per layer average absolute distance
    for i in range(len(f_fake)):
        loss_feat_match += K.mean(K.abs(f_fake[i] - f_real[i]))

    # scale the loss
    loss_feat_match *= feature_matching_weight
    return loss_feat_match
```

 Note that our implementation is slightly different than the equation previously described, but produces similar results.

The data used for pix2pixHD is different than pix2pix, so we need a new data-loading function that includes computing edge boundaries from instance maps. The training signature for pix2pixHD is also slightly different from the signature used on pix2pix. We provide the annotated code in our GitHub repository.

Let's now look at the training loop.

Training setup

The training setup for pix2pixHD is complex given the number of entities and the dependencies between them. We need to instantiate variables for the different types of input (segmentation maps, images, and instance boundaries), and we need to handle multiple Discriminators and the feature matching loss function. Let's start with the initializations and look at the code step by step:

1. Instantiate the logger and add learning rate scalars:

```
logger = SummaryWriter(out_dir)
logger.add_scalar('d_lr', lr_d, 0)
logger.add_scalar('g_lr', lr_g, 0)
```

2. Instantiate training and validation data:

```
data_iterator = iterate_minibatches_cityscapes(
data_folderpath, "train", use_edges, batch_size)
val_data_iterator = iterate_minibatches_cityscapes(
data_folderpath, "train", use_edges, n_checkpoint_samples)
```

3. Instantiate fixed data for evaluation:

```
input_val, _ = next(val_data_iterator)
img_fixed = input_val[..., :3]
lbl_fixed = input_val[..., 3][..., None]
edges_fixed = input_val[..., 4][..., None]
```

4. Instantiate and report data shapes:

```
img_shape = img_fixed.shape[1:]
lbl_shape = lbl_fixed.shape[1:]
edges_shape = edges_fixed.shape[1:]
h_patch = int(lbl_shape[0] / 2**3) # n_layers
w_patch = int(lbl_shape[1] / 2**3) # n_layers
disc_patch_0 = (h_patch, w_patch, 1)
disc_patch_1 = (int(h_patch/2), int(w_patch/2), 1)
disc_patch_2 = (int(h_patch/4), int(w_patch/4), 1)
print("img shape ", img_shape)
print("lbl shape ", lbl_shape)
print("edges shape ", edges_shape)
print("disc_patch ", disc_patch_0)
print("disc_patch ", disc_patch_1)
print("disc_patch ", disc_patch_2)
```

5. Plot real data for reference:

```
plot_dims = int(np.sqrt(img_fixed.shape[0]))
log_images(img_fixed, 'real_img', '0', logger, img_fixed.shape[1],
           img_fixed.shape[2], plot_dims)
log_images(lbl_fixed, 'real_lbls', '0', logger, img_fixed.shape[1],
           img_fixed.shape[2], plot_dims)
log_images(edges_fixed, 'real_edges', '0', logger,
img_fixed.shape[1],
           img_fixed.shape[2], plot_dims)
```

6. Build the Discriminators:

```
D0 = build_discriminator(lbl_shape, img_shape, edges_shape, ndf,
                         activation='linear', n_downsampling=0,
                         name='Discriminator0')
D1 = build_discriminator(lbl_shape, img_shape, edges_shape, ndf,
                         activation='linear', n_downsampling=1,
                         name='Discriminator1')
D2 = build_discriminator(lbl_shape, img_shape, edges_shape, ndf,
                         activation='linear', n_downsampling=2,
                         name='Discriminator2')
```

7. Build the Generator:

```
G = build_global_generator(lbl_shape, edges_shape, ngf)
```

8. Instantiate model inputs and outputs:

```
lbl_input = Input(shape=lbl_shape)
img_input = Input(shape=img_shape)
edges_input = Input(shape=edges_shape)
fake_samples = G([lbl_input, edges_input])[0]
```

9. Get Discriminator outputs, not including the intermediate outputs:

```
D0_real = D0([lbl_input, img_input, edges_input])[0]
D0_fake = D0([lbl_input, fake_samples, edges_input])[0]
D1_real = D1([lbl_input, img_input, edges_input])[0]
D1_fake = D1([lbl_input, fake_samples, edges_input])[0]
D2_real = D2([lbl_input, img_input, edges_input])[0]
D2_fake = D2([lbl_input, fake_samples, edges_input])[0]
```

10. Define a graph and optimizer for the Discriminators, including LSGAN `loss` (`mse`):

```
G.trainable = False
D0.trainable = True
D1.trainable = True
D2.trainable = True
D0_model = Model([lbl_input, img_input, edges_input], [D0_real,
D0_fake],
                   name='Discriminator0_model')
D1_model = Model([lbl_input, img_input, edges_input], [D1_real,
D1_fake],
                   name='Discriminator1_model')
D2_model = Model([lbl_input, img_input, edges_input], [D2_real,
D2_fake],
                   name='Discriminator2_model')
D0_model.compile(optimizer=Adam(lr_d, beta_1=0.5, beta_2=0.999),
                   loss=['mse', 'mse'])
D1_model.compile(optimizer=Adam(lr_d, beta_1=0.5, beta_2=0.999),
                   loss=['mse', 'mse'])
D2_model.compile(optimizer=Adam(lr_d, beta_1=0.5, beta_2=0.999),
                   loss=['mse', 'mse'])
```

11. Define the $D(G(z))$ loss, graph, and optimizer:

```
G.trainable = True
D0.trainable = False
D1.trainable = False
D2.trainable = False
```

12. Define symbolic inputs for the feature matching loss:

```
loss_fm0 = partial(loss_feature_matching, lbl_map=lbl_input,
                   real_samples=img_input, edges_map=edges_input,
D=D0,
                   feature_matching_weight=feature_matching_weight)
loss_fm1 = partial(loss_feature_matching, lbl_map=lbl_input,
                   real_samples=img_input, edges_map=edges_input,
D=D1,
                   feature_matching_weight=feature_matching_weight)
loss_fm2 = partial(loss_feature_matching, lbl_map=lbl_input,
                   real_samples=img_input, edges_map=edges_input,
D=D2,
                   feature_matching_weight=feature_matching_weight)
```

13. Define G inputs and outputs, including LSGAN `loss` (mse) and feature matching losses:

```
G_model = Model(
 inputs=[lbl_input, img_input, edges_input],
 outputs=[D0_fake, D1_fake, D2_fake, fake_samples, fake_samples,
fake_samples])
 G_model.compile(Adam(lr=lr_g, beta_1=0.5, beta_2=0.999),
 loss=['mse', 'mse', 'mse', loss_fm0, loss_fm1, loss_fm2])
```

14. Instantiate variables for computing the loss:

```
ones_0 = np.ones((batch_size, ) + disc_patch_0, dtype=np.float32)
ones_1 = np.ones((batch_size, ) + disc_patch_1, dtype=np.float32)
ones_2 = np.ones((batch_size, ) + disc_patch_2, dtype=np.float32)
zeros_0 = np.zeros((batch_size, ) + disc_patch_0, dtype=np.float32)
zeros_1 = np.zeros((batch_size, ) + disc_patch_1, dtype=np.float32)
zeros_2 = np.zeros((batch_size, ) + disc_patch_2, dtype=np.float32)
dummy = np.ones((batch_size, ), dtype=np.float32)
```

Now that we have instantiated the necessary things for training our models, we can finally look at the training loop.

Training loop

The training loop for pix2pixHD is very similar to pix2pix, with the exception that it uses more inputs than pix2pixHD. In addition, pix2pixHD has more losses than pix2pix, which requires us to include a new loss plotting function:

```
# training loop
for i in range(n_iterations):
    # train discriminators only
    D0.trainable = True
    D1.trainable = True
    D2.trainable = True
    G.trainable = False

    # sample batch of data and assign them to readable variables
    batch, _ = next(data_iterator)
    img = batch[..., :3]
    segmap = batch[..., 3][..., None]
    edges = batch[..., 4][..., None]
    fake_image = G.predict([segmap, edges])[0]

    # compute discriminators' loss on current batch
    loss_d0 = D0_model.train_on_batch([segmap, img, edges],
```

```
        [ones_0, zeros_0])
        loss_d1 = D1_model.train_on_batch([segmap, img, edges],
        [ones_1, zeros_1])
        loss_d2 = D2_model.train_on_batch([segmap, img, edges],
        [ones_2, zeros_2])

        # train generator only
        D0.trainable = False
        D1.trainable = False
        D2.trainable = False
        G.trainable = True

        # sample batch of data
        batch, _ = next(data_iterator)
        img = batch[..., :3]
        segmap = batch[..., 3][..., None]
        edges = batch[..., 4][..., None]

        # compute loss on current batch
        loss_g = G_model.train_on_batch(
        [segmap, img, edges],
        [ones_0, ones_1, ones_2, dummy, dummy, dummy])

        # logs results
        print("iter", i)
        if (i % iters_per_checkpoint) == 0:
            G.trainable = False
            fake_image = G.predict([lbl_fixed, edges_fixed])[0]
            log_images(fake_image, 'val_fake', i, logger,
            fake_image.shape[1], fake_image.shape[2],
            int(np.sqrt(fake_image.shape[0])))
            save_model(G, out_dir)
            log_losses_pix2pixhd([loss_d0, loss_d1, loss_d2], loss_g,
    i, logger)
```

After a few hours of training this model, you should be able to produce images like the following:

The quality of the images produced by the Generator will improve as training progresses.

Summary

In this chapter, we learned how to use the GAN framework to build models that can be used to synthesize and manipulate images conditioned on other images, also known as image-to-image translation. We started from a pix2pix baseline implementation and trained a model using the Zappos dataset to synthesize images of shoes from shoe outlines. In pix2pix, we did not use a z vector on the Generator and variety was obtained by using dropout. Unlike Discriminators that we have seen in previous chapters, pix2pix uses a PatchGAN Discriminator that outputs multiple values per image.

We then learned how to improve the baseline implementation by making many of the modifications proposed in the pix2pixHD paper. The first modification was to use multi-scale Discriminators that operate on images at different resolutions. The second modification was the feature matching loss, which is believed to improve image quality. Implementing the feature matching loss in Keras is rather intricate, and this adds yet another powerful and valuable tool to our GAN toolkit. Finally, we used instance maps to compute instance edges, which were used to guide the Generator image synthesis process.

In the next chapter, we will learn about the progressive growth of GANs.

7
Progressive Growing of GANs

Progressive Growing of **Generative Adversarial Networks** (**GANs**) is a training methodology that is introduced in a context where high-resolution image synthesis was dominated by autoregressive models, such as PixelCNN and **Variational Autoencoders** (**VAEs**) – just like the models used in the paper *Improved Variational Inference with Inverse Autoregressive Flow* (https://arxiv.org/abs/1606.04934).

As we described in earlier chapters, although autoregressive models are able to produce high-quality images, when compared to their counterparts they lack an explicit latent representation that can be directly manipulated. Additionally, due to their autoregressive nature, at the time of inference autoregressive models tend to be slower than their counterparts. On the other hand, VAE-based models have quicker inference but are harder to train, and the VAE-based models that have been published tend to produce blurry results.

In this mix of models, we also have GANs that, at the time, were not able to produce high-quality images with large resolutions such as 1024 by 1024. In addition to this limitation, producing samples with enough variety was a common problem that GAN models faced. Completing the list of GAN issues were the long training times and high sensitivity to hyperparameter initializations.

In this chapter, you will learn how to implement *Progressive Growing of GANs for Improved Quality, Stability, and Variation* by Tero Karras et al; this is a new training methodology in which the generator and discriminator are trained progressively. Starting from low-resolution images, we will then add new layers that model increasingly fine details as the training process progresses and the image resolution increases. These speeds up the training process and stabilizes it, allowing us to produce images of unprecedented quality. We will explore in detail how the authors increase variety by using minibatch standard deviation and how they normalize the generator and discriminator for training stability. We will run our experiments on the CIFAR 10 dataset with a model and training setup that is easy to adapt to other datasets, such as CelebA.

The following topics will be covered in this chapter:

- Progressive Growing of GANs
- Experimental setup
- Model implementation

Technical requirements

In this chapter, we will focus on the CIFAR 10 dataset that is available in Keras.

We will rely on the software libraries included in our Docker container, which are available at `https://github.com/packt/hands_on_gans_with_keras/blob/master/Dockerfile`.

You can visit the GitHub repository of this book for the full code files at `https://github.com/PacktPublishing/Hands-On-Generative-Adversarial-Networks-with-Keras`.

Progressive Growing of GANs

Progressive Growing of GANs offers a methodology that circumvents many of the problems related to GANs. It was the first publication to produce CelebA images using a resolution of 1024 by 1024; this was a task that was very challenging at the time the paper was published:

Samples generated with Progressive Growing of GANs. Source: *Progressive Growing of GANs for Improved Quality, Stability and Variation.* https://arxiv.org/pdf/1710.10196.pdf

As the name suggests, the methodology used in Progressive Growing of GANs consists of gradually increasing the resolution of the inputs, in this case, images, which are being handled or synthesized by the discriminator and generator. Likewise, layers are added to the discriminator and the generator in order to support higher resolutions.

In practice, instead of adding layers, a user defines the full graph of the discriminator and the generator and then selects the proper output with respect to the current level of detail (lod) being trained.

The methodology used in Progressive Growing of GANs is related to a broader methodology called curriculum learning. Here, easier concepts are introduced before hard concepts. In the context of Progressive Growing of GANs, images at a lower resolution are easier to synthesize than images at a higher resolution.

In summary, Progressive Growing of GANs is a training methodology that speeds up and stabilizes the training of GANs.

Increasing variation using minibatch standard deviation

In their paper, Tero Karras et al. propose a replacement for minibatch discrimination that uses no learnable parameters or new hyperparameters. Minibatch discrimination adds a layer toward the end of the discriminator that computes statistics across the minibatch. These obtained statistics are concatenated to the discriminator's output, allowing the discriminator to use the statistics explicitly.

Tero's replacement is simple and efficient and is also introduced toward the end of the discriminator. In their paper, they describe a solution that uses the average of the standard deviations computed for each feature on each spatial location in the minibatch. This operation produces a single value that will be concatenated, in a similar way to minibatch discrimination, to the discriminator's output.

Although one could vote for using more in their experiments, the authors found that using more statistics does not improve variation further.

Normalization in the generator and the discriminator

In their paper, Tero Karras et al. describe an unexpected approach for weight initialization that goes against the current trend of carefully initializing the weights of GAN models. Their approach is simple and fast: they initialize the weights from a normal distribution with a mean of 0 and a standard deviation of 1, and then scale the weights using a per-layer normalization constant. That is, given the w_i weight and the per-layer normalization c constant, the weights become $\hat{w}_i = w_i/c$.

Pixelwise feature vector normalization in the generator

As the name suggests, the authors normalize the feature vectors to the unit norm after each convolution layer in the generator. They claim that, by applying feature vector normalization, the escalation of signal magnitudes is prevented.

In practice, they use an adaptation of the local response normalization approach by Krizhevsky and others, which was published in 2012. Taking into account all feature maps, N, the feature vectors, $a_{x,y}$, are, therefore, normalized according to the following equation:

$$b_{x,y} = a_{x,y} / \sqrt{\frac{1}{N} \sum_{j=0}^{N-1} (a_{x,y}^j)^2 + \epsilon}$$

Experimental setup

In this section, we are going to implement training functions that are compatible with the Progressive Growing of GANs methodology. These training and logging functions will be used to train the discriminator and the generator, which will also be implemented in this section.

We will also implement helper functions in order to make it easier to compute our loss function based on the Wasserstein GAN with Gradient Penalty.

Training

Our training method consists of the following two parts:

- Initializing the required variables and compiling models
- The training loop itself

We will start by looking at the training layout:

```
def train(n_channels=3, resolution=32, z_dim=128, n_labels=0, lr=1e-3,
          e_drift=1e-3, wgp_target=750, initial_resolution=4,
    total_kimg=20000,
          training_kimg=400, transition_kimg=400, iters_per_checkpoint=500,
          n_checkpoint_images=16, glob_str='cifar10', out_dir='cifar10'):
```

Let's examine each argument of our `train` method in the following table:

Argument	Description
n_channels	The number of image channels
resolution	The target image resolution
z_dim	The size of the latent vector
n_labels	The number of labels
lr	The learning rate for the discriminator and the generator
batch_size	The batch size
e_drift	Epsilon scale for drift loss
wgp_target	Wassertein Gradient Penalty target
initial_resolution,	The image resolution at the beginning
total_kimg, training_kimg, transition_kimg	The number of total images, training images, and transition images in thousands
iters_per_checkpoint, n_checkpoints_per-image	The number of checkpoints per image
data	The string for matching data; this can be cifar10 or celeba
out_dir	The path to the directory where the outputs will be saved

Helper functions

The following functions are helper functions that can be used while computing the Wasserstein GAN loss with Gradient Penalty.

The first function is as follows:

```
def get_interpolated_images(real_samples, fake_samples):
    p = np.random.uniform(0, 1, size=(real_samples.shape[0], 1, 1, 1))
    return p * real_samples + (1-p) * fake_samples
```

The next three functions are necessary for computing the generator's loss, which is the negative average of the discriminator's output on fake samples, and to compute the discriminator's Wasserstein distance and penalty terms. In this implementation, we take advantage of the fact that the expected value is a linear operator and, therefore, we take the mean of the differences instead of the difference of the means:

```
def identity(y_true, y_pred):
    return y_pred


def loss_gradient_penalty(gamma, y_pred):
    return K.mean(K.square(y_pred - gamma) / K.square(gamma))


def loss_scaled_mean(y_true, y_pred):
    return K.mean(y_true*y_pred)
```

Now let's take a look at a few variables and model instantiations.

Initializations

The following are the steps:

1. Similar to most GAN training setups, we instantiate iterators to load data, build the discriminator and generator, and then compile the discriminator and generator that will be used during training, including defining their loss functions and optimizers.
2. First, instantiate the `logger`, as follows:

    ```
    logger = SummaryWriter(out_dir)
    ```

3. Then, load the `data`, as follows:

    ```
    batch_size = MINIBATCH_OVERWRITES[0]
    train_data, val_data = get_data(data)
    train_iterator = iterate_minibatches(train_data, batch_size)
    val_iterator = iterate_minibatches(val_data,
n_checkpoint_images)
    ```

4. Next, build the models, as follows:

```
D = Discriminator(n_channels, resolution, n_labels)
G = Generator(n_channels, resolution, n_labels)

G_train, D_train = GAN(G, D, z_dim, n_labels, resolution,
n_channels)

D_opt = Adam(lr=lr, beta_1=0.0, beta_2=0.99, epsilon=1e-8)
G_opt = Adam(lr=lr, beta_1=0.0, beta_2=0.99, epsilon=1e-8)
```

5. Define the loss functions, as follows:

```
D_loss =[identity, loss_gradient_penalty, 'mse']
G_loss = [loss_scaled_mean]
```

6. Compile the graphs that were used during training, as follows:

```
G.compile(G_opt, loss=loss_scaled_mean)
D.trainable = False
G_train.compile(G_opt, loss=G_loss)
D.trainable = True
D_train.compile(D_opt, loss=D_loss, loss_weights=[1, GP_WEIGHT,
e_drift])
```

7. For computing the loss later, we instantiate the following variables:

```
ones = np.ones((batch_size, 1), dtype=np.float32)
zeros = ones * 0.0
```

8. Fix a z vector for the training evaluation and setup initial variables, as follows:

```
z_fixed = np.random.normal(0, 1, size=(n_checkpoint_images,
z_dim))

# vars
resolution_log2 = int(np.round(np.log2(G.output_shape[2])))
starting_block = resolution_log2
starting_block -= np.floor(np.log2(initial_resolution))
cur_block = starting_block
```

9. Compute the duration of each phase and use a proxy in order to update the minibatch size and level of detail:

```
phase_kdur = training_kimg + transition_kimg
phase_idx_prev = 0

# offset variable for transitioning between blocks
```

```
offset = 0
cur_nimg = 0
i = 0
```

Now let's take a look at the training loop itself.

Training loops

Unlike traditional GAN setups, the training loop for the Progressive Growing of GANs methodology requires transitioning from a block of lower resolution to a block of a higher resolution. Given that blocks at lower resolution consume less memory, we can also modify the batch size according to the current block at hand:

```
while cur_nimg < total_kimg * 1000:
    # block processing
    kimg = cur_nimg / 1000.0
    phase_idx = int(np.floor((kimg + transition_kimg) /
phase_kdur))
    phase_idx = max(phase_idx, 0.0)
    phase_kimg = phase_idx * phase_kdur

    # update batch size and ones vector if we switched phases
    if phase_idx_prev < phase_idx:
        batch_size = MINIBATCH_OVERWRITES[phase_idx]
        train_iterator = iterate_minibatches(glob_str,
batch_size)
        ones = np.ones((batch_size, 1), dtype=np.float32)
        zeros = ones * 0.0
        phase_idx_prev = phase_idx

    # possibly gradually update current level of detail
    if transition_kimg > 0 and phase_idx > 0:
        offset = (kimg + transition_kimg - phase_kimg) /
transition_kimg
        offset = min(offset, 1.0)
        offset = offset + phase_idx - 1
        cur_block = max(starting_block - offset, 0.0)

    # update level of detail
    K.set_value(G_train.cur_block, np.float32(cur_block))
    K.set_value(D_train.cur_block, np.float32(cur_block))

    # train D
    for j in range(N_CRITIC_ITERS):
        z = np.random.normal(0, 1, size=(batch_size, z_dim))
        real_batch = next(train_iterator)
```

```
            fake_batch = G.predict_on_batch([z])
            interpolated_batch = get_interpolated_images(
                real_batch, fake_batch)
            losses_d = D_train.train_on_batch(
                [real_batch, fake_batch, interpolated_batch],
                [ones, ones*wgp_target, zeros])
            cur_nimg += batch_size

        # train G
        z = np.random.normal(0, 1, size=(batch_size, z_dim))
        loss_g = G_train.train_on_batch(z, -1*ones)

        logger.add_scalar("cur_block", cur_block, i)
        logger.add_scalar("learning_rate", lr, i)
        logger.add_scalar("batch_size", z.shape[0], i)
        print("iter", i, "cur_block", cur_block, "lr", lr, "kimg",
kimg,
            "losses_d", losses_d, "loss_g", loss_g)
        if (i % iters_per_checkpoint) == 0:
            G.trainable = False
            fake_images = G.predict(z_fixed)
            # log fake images
            print("fake min", fake_images.min(), "fake_max",
fake_images.max())
            log_images(fake_images, 'fake', i, logger,
                    fake_images.shape[1], fake_images.shape[2],
                    int(np.sqrt(n_checkpoint_images)))

            # plot real images for reference
            log_images(real_batch[:n_checkpoint_images], 'real', i,
logger,
                    real_batch.shape[1], real_batch.shape[2],
                    int(np.sqrt(n_checkpoint_images)))

            # save the model to eventually resume training or do
inference
            save_model(G, out_dir+"/model.json",
out_dir+"/model.h5")

        log_losses(losses_d, loss_g, i, logger)
        i += 1


train()
```

Model implementation

Implementing the models for Progressive Growing of GANs is a complex task, as the models have many custom layers and operations that are not implemented out of the box, including layers to perform pixel normalization, weight normalization during runtime, and more.

In addition to these layers, in our model design, we are including a mechanism in the models themselves; this allows for the runtime evaluation of the block that will be used as a model output, including how much input it receives from the previous layer.

The implementation described in this book, which encourages code reuse, uses (or adapts) code from an excellent implementation made by the *Microsoft's Student Club of Beihang University* group (https://github.com/MSC-BUAA/Keras-progressive_growing_of_gans/tree/master/Progressive%20growing%20of%20GANs).

Custom layers

Let's take a look at the many custom layers and helper functions that are used in our Progressive Growing of GANs implementation. We are going to cover the MinibatchStatConcatLayer layer, which computes statistics that are used on the last layers of the discriminator; the WeightScalingLayer layer, which scales the weights by their L2 norm; the PixelNormLayer layer, which scales the activations; the BlockSelectionLayer layer, which chooses the model output with respect to the current level of detail; and the ResizeLayer layer, which rescales the activations.

The custom layers that we are going to write will overwrite four methods at most, including _init_, build, call, and compute_output_shape.

We will start with the MinibatchStatConcatLayer layer.

```
class MinibatchStatConcatLayer(Layer):
    def __init__(self, group_size=1, **kwargs):
        super(MinibatchStatConcatLayer, self).__init__(**kwargs)
        self.group_size = int(group_size)

    def call(self, x):
        # standard deviation over minibatch n for each feature and
location
        y = K.sqrt(K.mean(K.square(x - K.mean(x, axis=0,
keepdims=True)),
                          axis=0, keepdims=True) + 1e-8)
```

```
        # compute the mean standard deviation
        y = K.mean(y, keepdims=True)

        # repeat to match n, h and w and have 1 feature map
        x_shape = K.shape(x)
        y = K.tile(y, [x_shape[0], x_shape[1], x_shape[2], 1])

        return K.concatenate([x, y], axis=-1)

    def compute_output_shape(self, input_shape):
        # output shape is input shape plus one feature map
        input_shape = list(input_shape)
        input_shape[-1] += 1
        return tuple(input_shape)
```

Now we will look at the `WeightScalingLayer` layer, which simply scales the kernel weights using a scalar value:

```
class WeightScalingLayer(Layer):
    def __init__(self, shape, gain=np.sqrt(2), **kwargs):
        super(WeightScalingLayer, self).__init__(**kwargs)
        fan_in = np.prod(shape[:-1])
        std = gain / np.sqrt(fan_in)

        # add the scale term as a non-trainable parameter
        self.wscale = self.add_weight(name='wscale',
shape=std.shape,
                                    trainable=False,
initializer='zeros')
        K.set_value(self.wscale, std)

    def call(self, input, **kwargs):
        # here scaling the layer outputs is equivalent to scaling
the weights
        return input * self.wscale

    def compute_output_shape(self, input_shape):
        return input_shape
```

Then, we will look at yet another scaling layer, the `PixelNormLayer` layer, which scales the inputs by the L2 norm:

```
class PixelNormLayer(Layer):
    def __init__(self, **kwargs):
        super(PixelNormLayer, self).__init__(**kwargs)

    def call(self, x, eps=1e-8, **kwargs):
        # we use rqrt(reciprocal square root) for faster
```

```
computation
        return x * tf.rsqrt(K.mean(K.square(x), axis=-1,
keepdims=True) + eps)

    def compute_output_shape(self, input_shape):
        return input_shape
```

We now look at the `BlockSelectionLayer` layer; this is the layer that we use to choose which layer will produce the model outputs. In this setup, earlier layers handle lower resolutions while later layers handle higher resolutions:

```
class BlockSelectionLayer(Layer):
    def __init__(self, cur_block, first_incoming_block=0,
ref_idx=0,
                min_block=None, max_block=None):
        super(BlockSelectionLayer, self).__init__()
        # instantiate attributes to be used during training
        self.cur_block = cur_block
        self.first_incoming_block = first_incoming_block
        self.ref_idx = ref_idx
        self.min_block = min_block
        self.max_block = max_block

    def call(self, inputs):
        # collect input shapes and resize data to match reference
shape
        self.input_shapes = [K.int_shape(input) for input in
inputs]
        v = [ResizeLayer(K.int_shape(input),
            self.input_shapes[self.ref_idx])(input) for input in
inputs]

        # possibly define lowest block based on minimum block
        if self.min_block is not None:
            min_from_first = self.min_block -
self.first_incoming_block
            min_from_first = int(np.floor(min_from_first))
            lo = np.clip(min_from_first, 0, len(v) - 1)
        else:
            lo = 0
        # possibly define highest block based on maximum block
        if self.max_block is not None:
            max_from_first = self.max_block -
self.first_incoming_block
            max_from_first = int(np.ceil(max_from_first))
            hi = np.clip(max_from_first, lo, len(v) - 1)
        else:
            hi = len(v) - 1
```

```
# set target block t and result r to highest output v[hi]
t = self.cur_block - self.first_incoming_block
r = v[hi]

# iterate over blocks
for i in range(hi-1, lo-1, -1): # i = hi-1, hi-2, ..., lo
    # while target block t is not reached update r with the
    interpolated value
    r = K.switch(K.less(t, i+1), v[i] * ((i+1)-t) + v[i+1]
* (t-i), r)

# if target block is smaller than min block lo return min
block else keep r
if lo < hi:
    r = K.switch(K.less_equal(t, lo), v[lo], r)

return r
```

Finally, we look at the `ResizeLayer` layer, which resizes the activations such that we can scale our inputs to transition from one resolution to another by using average pooling when decreasing the size of the inputs and repeating elements when increasing the size of the inputs:

```
class ResizeLayer(Layer):
    def __init__(self, input_dims, output_dims, **kwargs):
        self.input_dims = input_dims
        self.output_dims = output_dims
        super(ResizeLayer, self).__init__(**kwargs)

    def call(self, v, **kwargs):
        assert (len(self.input_dims) == len(self.output_dims) and
                self.input_dims[0] == self.output_dims[0])

        # possibly shrink spatial axis by pooling elements
        if len(self.input_dims) == 4 and (self.input_dims[1] >
self.output_dims[1] or self.input_dims[2] > self.output_dims[2]):
            assert (self.input_dims[1] % self.output_dims[1] == 0
and
                self.input_dims[2] % self.output_dims[2] == 0)

            pool_sizes = (self.input_dims[1] / self.output_dims[1],
                          self.input_dims[2] / self.output_dims[2])
            strides = pool_sizes
            v = K.pool2d(
                v, pool_size=pool_sizes, strides=strides,
                padding='same', data_format='channels_last',
pool_mode='avg')
```

```
            # possibly extend spatial axis by repeating elements
            for i in range(1, len(self.input_dims) - 1):
                if self.input_dims[i] < self.output_dims[i]:
                    assert self.output_dims[i] % self.input_dims[i] ==
0
                    v = K.repeat_elements(
                        v, rep=int(self.output_dims[i] /
self.input_dims[i]),
                            axis=i)

        return v

    def compute_output_shape(self, input_shape):
        return self.output_dims
```

The discriminator

The discriminator that is used in Progressive Growing of GANs consists of stacks of convolutions followed by downsampling layers. Each convolution has a WeightScalingLayer layer that normalizes the layer outputs using a constant, and a PixelNormLayer layer that normalizes the outputs by their L2 norm, thus ensuring that the outputs vector has unit length.

Specific to the Progressive Growing of GANs methodology, this discriminator architecture has a BlockSelectionLayer layer, which defines the layer that should be used as the output during training. Remember, in this methodology, we first train an output layer at a low resolution and then train the other layers that output a higher resolution one by one.

Another special addition to the discriminator is the MinibatchStatConcatLayer layer. This first computes the standard deviation for each feature, or channel, in each spatial location over the minibatch, and then takes the average standard deviation:

```
def Discriminator(n_channels=1, resolution=32, n_labels=0,
fmap_base=4096,
                  fmap_max=128):

    resolution_log2 = int(np.log2(resolution))
    assert resolution == 2 ** resolution_log2 and resolution >= 4
    cur_block = K.variable(np.float(0.0), dtype='float32')

    images_in = Input(shape=[resolution, resolution, n_channels])
    images = images_in

    # the first block has a 1x1 conv
    x = Conv1x1(images, n_filters(resolution_log2-1, fmap_base,
```

```
fmap_max),
                    use_activation=True)

    # subsequent blocks or stages
    block_inputs = []
    for i in range(resolution_log2-1, 1, -1):
        x = ConvBlock(x, n_filters(i, fmap_base, fmap_max), 3,
'same',
                    use_pixelnorm=False)
        x = ConvBlock(x, n_filters(i - 1, fmap_base, fmap_max), 3,
'same',
                    use_pixelnorm=False)
        x = DownsamplingLayer(factor=2)(x)
        block = DownsamplingLayer(factor=2 ** (resolution_log2-
i))(images)
        block = Conv1x1(block, n_filters(i - 1, fmap_base,
fmap_max),
                    use_activation=True)
        x = BlockSelectionLayer(
            cur_block, first_incoming_block=resolution_log2 - i -
1)([x, block])

    # compute and concatenate minibatch statistics
    x = MinibatchStatConcatLayer()(x)

    # last conv
    x = ConvBlock(x, n_filters(1, fmap_base, fmap_max), 3, 'same',
False)
    x = ConvBlock(x, n_filters(0, fmap_base, fmap_max), 4, 'valid',
False)

    # last dense block is linear
    outputs = DenseBlock(x, 1+n_labels, gain=1.0,
use_pixelnorm=False,
                    use_activation=False)

    # instantiate the model and current block
    model = Model(inputs=[images_in], outputs=outputs)
    model.cur_block = cur_block
    print('Discriminator')
    model.summary()
    return model
```

The generator

The generator that is used in Progressive Growing of GANs consists of stacks of convolutions followed by an upsampling layer. Each convolution has a `WeightScalingLayer` layer that normalizes the layer outputs with a constant, and a `PixelNormLayer` layer that normalizes the outputs by their L2 norm, thus ensuring that the outputs vector has unit length.

Specific to the Progressive Growing of GANs methodology, this generator architecture has a `BlockSelectionLayer` layer, which defines the layer that should be used as the output during training. Remember, in this methodology, we first train an output layer at a low resolution and then train the other layers that output a higher resolution one by one:

```
def Generator(n_channels=1, resolution=32, z_dim=512, n_labels=0,
              fmap_base=4096, fmap_max=128, normalize_z=True):
    # model setup
    resolution_log2 = int(np.log2(resolution))
    assert resolution == 2 ** resolution_log2 and resolution >= 4
    cur_block = K.variable(0.0, dtype='float32')

    # initialize z input
    z = Input(shape=[z_dim])

    # normalize z's such that they lay on a unit hypersphere
    x = PixelNormLayer()(z) if normalize_z else z

    # possibly concatenate z and labels
    inputs = z
    if n_labels:
        labels = Input(shape=[n_labels])
        inputs = [z, labels]
        x = Concatenate()([x, labels])

    # first block 4x4, sqrt(2)/4 as in github
    x = DenseBlock(x, n_filters(1, fmap_base, fmap_max)*4*4,
gain=np.sqrt(2)/4,
                   use_pixelnorm=True, use_activation=True,
                   reshape=(4, 4, n_filters(1, fmap_base,
fmap_max)))
    x = ConvBlock(x, n_filters(1, fmap_base, fmap_max), 3, 'same',
                  use_pixelnorm=True)

    # subsequent blocks or stages 8 x 8 and larger...
    block_activations = [x]
    for block in range(2, resolution_log2):
        x = UpsamplingLayer(factor=2)(x)
```

```
        x = ConvBlock(x, n_filters(block, fmap_base, fmap_max), 3,
    'same',
                          use_pixelnorm=True)
        x = ConvBlock(x, n_filters(block, fmap_base, fmap_max), 3,
    'same',
                          use_pixelnorm=True)
        block_activations.append(x)

    # compute the final output for each block
    block_outputs = [Conv1x1(1, n_channels, gain=1.0,
use_activation=False)
                     for l in reversed(block_activations)]

    # select the output block
    output = BlockSelectionLayer(cur_block)(block_outputs)

    # instantiate the model and current block
    model = Model(inputs=inputs, outputs=[output])
    model.cur_block = cur_block
    print('Generator')
    model.summary()
    return model
```

Now that we have written the code for both the discriminator and the generator, let's write a function that uses these models to return the models that will be used during training.

GANs

We wrap the generator and discriminator methods that are to be used during training in the following function:

```
def GAN(G, D, z_dim, n_labels, resolution, n_channels):
    # create D(G(z)) and set current block
    G_train = Sequential([G, D])
    G_train.cur_block = G.cur_block

    # instantiate symbolic variables for inputs
    shape = D.get_input_shape_at(0)[1:]
    gen_input, real_input = Input(shape), Input(shape)
    interpolation = Input(shape)

    # define the wasserstein distance and grad norm
    w_distance = WassersteinDistance()([D(gen_input),
D(real_input)])
    g_norm = GradNorm()([D(interpolation), interpolation])
    # use w_distance, g_norm and output of D on reals for computing
```

```
        the loss
        D_train = Model([real_input, gen_input, interpolation],
                        [w_distance, g_norm, Reshape((1,
))(D(real_input))])
        D_train.cur_block = D.cur_block

        return G_train, D_train
```

Note that this implementation is much cleaner than our previous implementation, as the Wasserstein GAN with Gradient Penalty loss is wrapped within the model.

Summary

In this chapter, we learned about the Progressive Growing of GANs architecture and how to implement it. We learned how to increase variation by using minibatch standard deviation, along with how to normalize the generator and discriminator for training stability.

In the next chapter, we will learn about the generation of discrete sequences using GANs.

8
Generation of Discrete Sequences Using GANs

In this chapter, you will learn how to implement a model that is used in the paper *Adversarial Generation of Natural Language* by Rajeswar et al. This model was first described in the paper Improved Training of Wasserstein GANs by Gulrajani et al. It is capable of generating short discrete sequences with small vocabularies.

We will first address language generation as a problem of conditional probability, in which we want to estimate the probability of the next token given the previous tokens. Then will address the challenges involved in training models for discrete sequences using GANs.

After this introduction to language generation, you will learn how to implement the model described in the paper by Rajeswar et al. and train it on the Google 1 Billion Word Dataset. We will train two separate models: one to generate sequences of characters and another to generate sequences of words.

The following topics will be covered in this chapter:

- Natural language generation with GANs
- Experimental setup
- Model implementation
- Inference

Technical requirements

The 1 Billion Word Dataset can be downloaded from `http://www.statmt.org/lm-benchmark/`.

We will rely on the software libraries included in our Docker container, available at `https://github.com/rafaelvalle/hands_on_gans_with_keras/blob/master/Dockerfile`.

You can visit this book's GitHub repository for the full code files: `https://github.com/PacktPublishing/Hands-On-Generative-Adversarial-Networks-with-Keras`.

Natural language generation with GANs

Within the field of **Natural language understanding** (NLU), Natural language generation is one of the most challenging tasks in machine learning. Broadly speaking, it is easier to estimate the parameters of a discriminative model than a generative model. On Quora (`https://www.quora.com/Why-are-generative-models-harder-to-create-than-discriminative-models`), Ian Goodfellow gives a good informal explanation that can be generalized to language:

> *Can you look at a painting and recognize it as being the Mona Lisa? You probably can. That's discriminative modeling. Can you paint the Mona Lisa yourself? You probably can't. That's generative modeling.*

The task of modeling language has been approached with rule-based and data-based models, including deep learning. As Ziang Xie has informally explained in his practical guide for neural text generation (`https://cs.stanford.edu/~zxie/textgen.pdf`), while deep learning models for neural text generation are very flexible and expressive at the price of being somewhat unpredictable and hard to control, conversely, rule-based models are predictable and easy to control but not very expressive nor flexible.

Until recently, a large body of natural language understanding models relied on n-gram language models. At scale, these models require prohibitive amounts of feature engineering and expert knowledge. Lately, approaching such problems with neural networks seem to be a viable end-to-end solution that reduces the dependency on feature engineering or on domain experts, at the cost of limited model interpretability and predictability.

In autoregressive models for language generation, the task of language generation is defined as the problem of predicting a token given the previously predicted tokens. As we saw in an earlier chapter, this formulation can be generalized to time-series from other domains. In Chapter 10, *Speech Enhancement with GANs*, we will revisit this formulation in the audio domain. This approach is very interesting because it fully models the dependencies between the tokens in the sentence or time-series.

Mathematically speaking, in autoregressive models, language generation is modeled by learning the distribution of the sentence, x, by factorizing it with the product of conditional probabilities:

$$P(x) = P(x_1, x_2, \ldots, x_T) = P(x_1)P(x2|x_1)P(x_3|x_2, x_1)\ldots P(x_T|x_1, \ldots, x_{t-1})$$
$$= \prod_{t=1}^{T} P(x_t|x_1, \ldots, x_{t-1})$$

The GAN approach to language generation is rather different from the auto-regressive approach we just described. The first challenge in using GANs is that during sampling, the output produced by the generator is a sequence of one-hot vectors that are not differentiable with respect to the weights of the generator. In this context, the derivative is 0 almost everywhere and infinite on the index containing 1. This is an issue because a small change in the weights will either result in no change to the output or in a change that will tend to be infinity.

Another challenge is that although recurrent neural networks are appropriate for fitting sequential problems, they are very hard to train using GANs. A way to circumvent this problem is to build a stack of Convolutions that operate like an n-gram.

The paper *Natural Language Generation with GANs* by Rajeswar et al. investigates different GANs and their uses in sequence generation. The authors circumvent the problem of discrete generator output by using the distribution output by the generator instead of the sampling that is taking the *argmax* of these values. Surprisingly, the authors were able to train their GAN-based text-generation models using both RNNs and Convolutions. The convolutional approach was described in the paper Improved Wasserstein GANs by Gulrajani et al. which was the first paper to perform discrete sequence generation with GANs.

The setup described in the paper is very similar to the traditional GAN setup, with the exception of the modification we mentioned earlier, in which the Softmax-ed output of the generator is used as input to the Discriminator. The following is a diagram provided by Rajeswar et al. in their paper on arXiv:

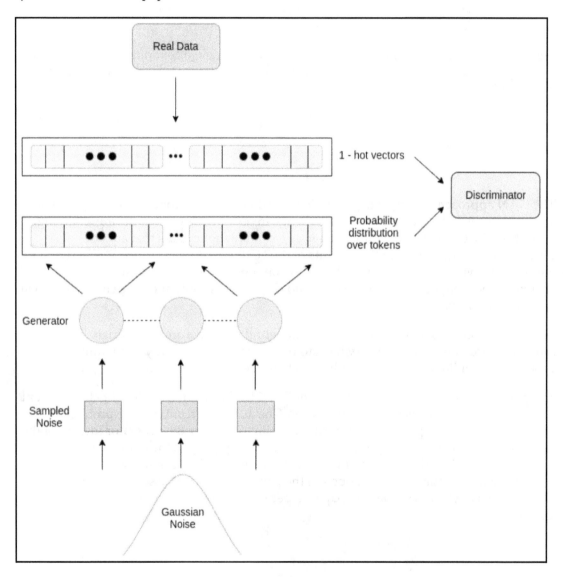

Natural Language Generation with GANs model architecture. Source: Adversarial Generation of Natural Language(https://arxiv.org/abs/1705.10929)

Experimental setup

In this section, we will start by implementing methods that are necessary for preparing and loading our data during training. Next, we will learn to implement auxiliary functions that are required for the Wasserstein GAN with Gradient Penalty. Last, we are going to write code to set up training and the training loop itself.

Data

We will focus on the 1-Billion Word *dataset* that was proposed in 2013 in the paper *One Billion Word Benchmark for Measuring Progress in Statistical Language Modeling* by Ciprian Chelba et al. This dataset can be downloaded from `http://www.statmt.org/lm-benchmark/`.

We will start with the imports, which include the libraries and functions in this subsection:

```
from collections import defaultdict, Counter
import numpy as np
from glob import glob
import pandas as pd
```

Now, we are going to define the method that loads the text data from disk and preprocesses it. The function signature includes variables to handle the start of the sentence (`sos`), the end of the sentence (`eos`), and unknown (`unk_token`) tokens:

```
def get_data(glob_str, vocabulary_size=96, sos="<s>", eos="</s>",
unk_token='|',
                            symbol_based=True,
max_number_sentences=500000):

    print("Loading data")
    data = None
    i = 0

    # use the glob_str to find all files matching the pattern
    for filepath in glob(glob_str):
        # read all lines at once
        with open(filepath) as f:
            cur_data = f.readlines()
```

Then we strip a new line symbol, convert in to lowercase, and add `sos` and `eos`:

```
if symbol_based:
        cur_data = [list(sos) + list(d.strip().lower()) + list(eos)
                    for d in cur_data]
    else:
        cur_data = [[sos] + d.strip().lower().split() + [eos]
                    for d in cur_data]
    data = cur_data if data is None else data + cur_data
```

Get the token `frequency` to prune uncommon tokens (words or characters) using the following code:

```
token_frequency = Counter(np.hstack(data))
token_frequency = pd.DataFrame.from_dict(
    token_frequency, orient='index', columns=['frequency'])
token_frequency = token_frequency.sort_values("frequency",
ascending=False)
```

Check whether the data has the unknown token: if not, create it:

```
unk_id = np.argwhere(token_frequency.index == unk_token)
if len(unk_id) > 0:
    unk_id = unk_id[0, 0]
else:
    unk_id = vocabulary_size - 1
    vocabulary_size -= 1

# drop tokens to have at most vocabulary_size number of tokens
token_frequency = token_frequency.drop(
    token_frequency.index[np.arange(vocabulary_size,
len(token_frequency))])
```

Create a map from the token to the ID and from the ID to the token using the following code:

```
token_to_id = defaultdict(lambda: unk_id)
id_to_token = defaultdict(lambda: unk_token)
token_to_id[unk_token] = unk_id
id_to_token[unk_id] = unk_token

for i, token in enumerate(token_frequency.index):
    token_to_id[token] = i
    id_to_token[i] = token

return data, token_to_id, id_to_token
```

Now, let's implement the common `iterate_minibatches` method:

```
def iterate_minibatches(data, token_to_id, vocabulary_size,
max_sentence_length,
                        batch_size=128):
    # we need a one hot matrix to encode the tokens into the one-hot
representation
    one_hot_matrix = np.eye(vocabulary_size)
    i = 0
    while True:
        # drop last?
        if len(data) - i*batch_size < batch_size or i == 0:
            ids = np.random.randint(0, len(data), len(data))
            np.random.shuffle(ids)
            i = 0
        # randomly select sentences and convert them to one-hot
        train_data = np.array([
            sentence_to_onehot(data[k], token_to_id, one_hot_matrix,
max_sentence_length)
            for k in ids[i*batch_size:(i+1)*batch_size]])
        i = (i + 1) % len(data)
        yield train_data
```

The following code has the `helper` function, which converts sentences to one-hot:

```
def sentence_to_onehot(sentence, token_to_id, one_hot_matrix,
                       max_sentence_length):
    # converts each token in the sentence to an id using the token to id map
    ids = [token_to_id[token] for token in sentence]

    # 'pad' shorter sentences to max_sentence_length
    if len(ids) < max_sentence_length:
      ids.extend([ids[-1]] * (max_sentence_length - len(ids)))

    # crop larger sentences to max_sentence_length
    ids = ids[:max_sentence_length]

    # use the ids to query the one-hot matrix
    return one_hot_matrix[ids][None, :]
```

This method uses the output of the generator and samples the IDs with the highest probability:

```
def sample(generator_output, id_to_token, join_char=' '):
    ids_per_batch = np.argmax(generator_output, axis=3)
    sentences = []
    for item in ids_per_batch:
        sentences.append(join_char.join([id_to_token[id] for id in
```

```
item[0]]))
    return sentences
```

Auxiliary training functions

We need to implement several functions to accommodate the Wasserstein GAN with Gradient Penalty loss. Our implementation is an adaptation of the implementation written by the Keras team; it can be found at https://github.com/keras-team/keras-contrib/blob/master/examples/improved_wgan.py

We start with the necessary imports:

```
import keras.backend as K
from keras.layers.merge import _Merge
```

We first define the Wasserstein loss, which is just the average of the Discriminator's output multiplied by the respective sign:

```
def loss_wasserstein(y_true, y_pred):
    return K.mean(y_true * y_pred)
```

Next, we define the Gradient Penalty loss:

```
def loss_gradient_penalty(y_true, y_pred, averaged_samples,
                          gradient_penalty_weight):
    # get gradients of D(averaged) wrt averaged. average between fake and
real data
    gradients = K.gradients(y_pred, averaged_samples)[0]

    # compute the euclidean norm, that is the square root of the sum of
squares:
    gradients_sqr = K.square(gradients)
    gradients_sqr_sum = K.sum(gradients_sqr, axis=np.arange(1,
len(gradients_sqr.shape)))
    gradient_l2_norm = K.sqrt(gradients_sqr_sum)

    # take the square distance from 1 and scale by lambda
    gradient_penalty = gradient_penalty_weight * K.square(gradient_l2_norm
- 1)
    # compute the mean
    return K.mean(gradient_penalty)
```

Finally, we use this auxiliary class to compute a random point between real and fake samples:

```
class RandomWeightedAverage(_Merge):
    def _merge_function(self, inputs):
        weights = K.random_uniform((BATCH_SIZE, 1, 1, 1))
        return (weights * inputs[0]) + ((1 - weights) * inputs[1])
```

Training

Our training method consists of three parts:

- Imports and initializing global variables
- Initializing the required variables and compiling the models
- The training loop

Imports and global variables

We will start with the imports and the global variables:

```
import numpy as np
from functools import partial
from keras.models import Model
from keras.layers import Input
from keras.optimizers import Adam
from keras.layers.merge import _Merge
from keras import backend as K
from models import (build_resnet_discriminator, build_resnet_generator)
from tensorboardX import SummaryWriter
from data_utils import get_data, iterate_minibatches, sample, log_text
from train_utils import loss_gradient_penalty, loss_wasserstein,
RandomWeightedAverage
N_CRITIC_ITERS = 10
GRADIENT_PENALTY_WEIGHT = 10
GLOB_STR = "data/1-billion-word-language-modeling-benchmark-
r13output/training-monolingual.tokenized.shuffled/*"
BATCH_SIZE = 0   # needed to compute the RandomWeightedAverage
```

Now we will take a look at the training method's signature:

```
def train(ndf=512, ngf=512, z_dim=128, n_residual_blocks_discriminator=5,
          n_residual_blocks_generator=5, lr_d=1e-4, lr_g=1e-4,
          n_iterations=int(1e6), batch_size=64, iters_per_checkpoint=2000,
          n_checkpoint_text=36, vocabulary_size=2048,
```

```
max_sentence_length=32,
        sos='<s>', eos='</s>', unk_token='<unk>', symbol_based=False,
        word_join=' ', out_dir='wgan_gp_word'):
```

Let's look at each argument of our `train` method in the following table:

Argument	Description
ndf, ngf	Number of discriminator and generator filters
n_residual_blocks_generator, n_residual_blocks_discriminator	Number of residual blocks for the generator and discriminator
lr_d, lr_g	Learning rate of the discriminator and generator
n_iterations, batch_size, iters_per_checkpoint, n_checkpoint_text	Self-descriptive
vocabulary_size	Maximum number of unique tokens
max_sentence_length	Maximum sentence length
sos, eos	Tokens for start of sentence, end of sentence
unk_token	Unknown token
word_join	Character to use to join words
symbol_based	Whether to use symbols or words
out_dir	Path to directory where output will be saved

Initializations

Let's implement the first part of our `train` method using the following steps:

1. Define a `global` batch for the Random Weighted Average calculation:

   ```
   global BATCH_SIZE
   BATCH_SIZE = batch_size
   ```

2. Instantiate the `logger` to save logs in `out_dir` and log learning rates of G and D:

   ```
   logger = SummaryWriter(out_dir)
   logger.add_scalar('d_lr', lr_d, 0)
   logger.add_scalar('g_lr', lr_g, 0)
   ```

3. Load the data and set up the mini-batch iterator:

   ```
   data, token_to_id, id_to_token = get_data(
           GLOB_STR, vocabulary_size, sos, eos, unk_token,
   symbol_based)
       data_iterator = iterate_minibatches(
   ```

```
                        data, token_to_id, vocabulary_size,
                   max_sentence_length, batch_size)
```

4. Sample real data, report the shape, and log the text for reference:

```
        real_sample = next(data_iterator)
          print("text shape {}".format(real_sample[0].shape))
          log_text(sample(real_sample, id_to_token, word_join), 'real',
        '0', logger)
```

5. Build models using the following code:

```
        input_shape_discriminator = text_shape
          input_shape_generator = (z_dim, )
          D = build_resnet_discriminator(
                  input_shape_discriminator, ndf,
        n_residual_blocks_discriminator)
          G = build_resnet_generator(
                  input_shape_generator, ngf,
        n_residual_blocks_generator,
                  max_sentence_length, vocabulary_size)
```

6. Build model outputs:

```
        real_inputs = Input(shape=real_sample.shape[1:])
          z = Input(shape=(z_dim, ))
          fake_samples = G(z)
          D_real = D(real_inputs)
          D_fake = D(fake_samples)

          # random weighted average between real and fake samples
          averaged_samples = RandomWeightedAverage()([real_inputs,
        fake_samples])

          # discriminator's output on real, fake and averaged samples
          D_real = D(real_inputs)
          D_fake = D(fake_samples)
          D_averaged = D(averaged_samples)
```

7. Instantiate the Gradient Penalty loss with the symbollic `averaged_samples` variable:

```
        loss_gp = partial(loss_gradient_penalty,
              averaged_samples=averaged_samples,
              gradient_penalty_weight=GRADIENT_PENALTY_WEIGHT)
```

8. Add a function name:

```
loss_gp.__name__ = 'loss_gradient_penalty'
```

9. Define the D graph and optimizer:

```
G.trainable = False
  D.trainable = True
  D_model = Model(inputs=[real_inputs, z],
      outputs=[D_real, D_fake, D_averaged])
  D_model.compile(optimizer=Adam(lr_d, beta_1=0.5, beta_2=0.9),
      loss=[loss_wasserstein, loss_wasserstein, loss_gp])
```

10. Define the D(G(z)) graph and optimizer:

```
G.trainable = True
  D.trainable = False
  G_model = Model(inputs=z, outputs=D_fake)
  G_model.compile(Adam(lr=lr_g, beta_1=0.5, beta_2=0.9),
      loss=loss_wasserstein)
```

11. Instantiate variables to compute the loss:

```
ones = np.ones((batch_size, 1), dtype=np.float32)
  minus_ones = -ones
  dummy = np.zeros((batch_size, 1), dtype=np.float32)
```

12. Fix a z vector for the training evaluation:

```
z_fixed = np.random.uniform(-1, 1, size=(n_checkpoint_text,
z_dim))
```

Training loop

To conclude, we define the training loop itself:

```
for i in range(n_iterations):
    # we are performing D updates only, fix G weights
    D.trainable = True
    G.trainable = False
    for j in range(N_CRITIC_ITERS):
        z = np.random.normal(0, 1, size=(batch_size, z_dim))
        real_batch = next(data_iterator)
        losses_d = D_model.train_on_batch(
            [real_batch, z], [minus_ones, ones, dummy])

    # we are performing G updates only, fix D weights
```

```
    D.trainable = False
    G.trainable = True
    z = np.random.normal(0, 1, size=(batch_size, z_dim))
    loss_g = G_model.train_on_batch(z, minus_ones)
    if (i % iters_per_checkpoint) == 0:
        G.trainable = False
        fake_text = G.predict(z_fixed)
        log_text(sample(fake_text, id_to_token, word_join), 'fake', i,
logger)
    log_losses(losses_d, loss_g, i, logger)


train()
```

Logging

For logging, we take advantage of Tensorboard's ability to log text by using the `.add_text` routine. This function takes as input the name of the tab associated with this text field, the text, and the iteration number:

```
def log_text(texts, name, i, logger):
    texts = '\n'.join(texts)
    logger.add_text('{}_{}'.format(name, i), texts, i)
```

For reporting losses, we include an extra `scalar` for the generator's reconstruction loss. The `add_scalar` function takes as input the name of the tab associated with this scalar field, the scalar value, and the iteration number. Note that the Wasserstein GAN with Gradient Penalty has an extra loss term related to the Gradient Penalty:

```
def log_losses(loss_d, loss_g, iteration, logger):
    names = ['loss_d', 'loss_d_real', 'loss_d_fake', 'loss_d_gp']
    for i in range(len(loss_d)):
        logger.add_scalar(names[i], loss_d[i], iteration)
        logger.add_scalar("losses_g", loss_g, iteration)
```

Model implementation

The Discriminator and generator models used in the paper are 1D Convolutions based on the ResNet architecture. We use 2D Convolutions with a singleton dimension for better computational performance.

Helper functions

We start with the necessary imports and initializations:

```
from keras.layers import Conv2D, Activation
from keras.layers import Add, Lambda
from keras.initializers import RandomNormal
weight_init = RandomNormal(mean=0., stddev=0.02)
```

Then we use the `helper` function that defines a ResNet block:

```
from keras.layers import Conv2D, Activation
from keras.layers import Add, Lambda
from keras.initializers import RandomNormal
weight_init = RandomNormal(mean=0., stddev=0.02)

def resnet_block(input, n_blocks, n_filters, kernel_size=(1, 3)):
    output = input
    for i in range(n_blocks):
        output = Activation('relu')(output)
        output = Conv2D(filters=n_filters, kernel_size=kernel_size,
                        strides=1, padding='same',
                        kernel_initializer=weight_init)(output)
        output = Activation('relu')(output)
        output = Conv2D(filters=n_filters, kernel_size=kernel_size, strides=1,
                        padding='same',
kernel_initializer=weight_init)(output)
        output = Lambda(lambda x: x * 0.3)(output)
        # Residual Connection
        output = Add()([input, output])
    return output
```

Discriminator

The Discriminator model consists of a Convolution followed by ResNet blocks and a dense layer that projects the learned features to a single number, as given in the following code block:

```
from keras.layers import Input, Flatten
from keras.layers import Dense, Conv2D
from keras.models import Model
def build_resnet_discriminator(input_shape, n_filters, n_residual_blocks,
                                kernel_size=(1, 1), stride=1):
    input = Input(shape=input_shape)
    x = Conv2D(filters=n_filters, kernel_size=kernel_size, strides=stride,
```

```
                    padding='same')(input)

    # resnet blocks
    x = resnet_block(x, n_residual_blocks, n_filters)

    # Flatten and project to a single dimension
    x = Flatten()(x)
    x = Dense(1)(x)
    # create model graph
    model = Model(inputs=input, outputs=x, name='Discriminator')
    print("\nDiscriminator ResNet")
    model.summary()
    return model
```

Generator

The generator model consists of a dense layer followed by ResNet blocks and a 2D Convolution layer with the Softmax non-linearity. The Softmax non-linearity normalizes the logits of the last layer to a probability distribution. Remember that, during training, no sampling step is required and the Softmax output is passed directly to the Discriminator:

```
from keras.layers import Input, Activation, Softmax
from keras.layers import Dense, Conv2D
from keras.layers.core import Reshape
from keras.models import Model

def build_resnet_generator(input_shape, n_filters, n_residual_blocks,
                           seq_len, vocabulary_size):
    inputs = Input(shape=input_shape)
    # Dense 1: 1 x seq_len x n_filters
    x = Dense(1 * seq_len * n_filters, input_shape=input_shape)(inputs)
    x = Reshape((1, seq_len, n_filters))(x)
    # ResNet blocks
    x = resnet_block(x, n_residual_blocks, n_filters)
    # Output layer
    x = Conv2D(filters=vocabulary_size, kernel_size=1, padding='same')(x)
    x = Softmax(axis=3)(x)

    # create model graph
    model = Model(inputs=inputs, outputs=x, name='Generator')
    print("\nGenerator ResNet")
    model.summary()
    return model
```

Inference

In this section, we are going to consider both our experimental setups: one where the generator and discriminator predict and discriminate sequences of words, and another where the models predict and discriminate sequences on characters. Note that in both cases, there is no difference between the representation of a word or a character; they are just vectors in multidimensional space.

Assuming the same sequence length, the task of predicting a sequence of characters is harder than the task of predicting a sequence of words. First, because in the character case the model has to perform more predictions. Second, because overall entropy or uncertainty when predicting characters is higher than predicting words, as it implies predicting a sequence of characters that form a word and predicting another sequence of characters that forms another word, and that is likely to be followed by the previously predicted word.

Although language is inherently sequential and words are, most of the time, samples conditioned on previous words, one is able to train an unconditional toy model of language with the GAN framework. Let's look at the output of the models trained to predict the sequence of words first.

Model trained on words

The code for sampling the generator is straightforward. First, we load the model, then create a z vector, get the output from the generator that provides the probability of each , also known as **logits**, and sample it with the mode of the distribution, that is, by taking the index with the highest probability and converting it into a word by using our `token_to_id` function:

```
import numpy as np
from utils import load_model, sample
def inference(model_path, weights_path):
    G = load_model(model_path, weights_path)
    z = np.random.uniform(-1, 1, 1)
    res = G.inference(z)
    text = sample(res)
    print(text)
```

In the following table, we provide cherry-picked examples that produce sequences of words that overall are grammatically and syntactically correct, although mistakes are still present. Note that the generator samples these words all at once and in-conditionally. <s>and </s> stand for start and end of phrase tokens:

<s> It 's Britain ? </s> </s> </s>
<s> But he has treatment majority -- the
<s> She really close and light . </s>
<s> And when we followed compared with Peter
<s> fact , think what you know ,
<s> I think you need to know ,
<s> " He could start up , of
<s> He said : " I think .
<s> No case or injuries , a score
<s> overall push . </s> </s> </s> </s>
<s> " What 's the choice UN and

In this table, we provide a list of not so successful examples that include syntax and grammar mistakes:

<s> " She did the source penalty ,
<s> But stopped could have to coach .
<s> The first Scottish were lot allowed something
<s> By 's fully be are book .
<s> This might tried 't that they have
<s> This seems to do executive had up
<s> " union you then to be five
<s> " She comment a biggest throughout .
<s> But vote to fact , we hit
<s> " Now it was this of a

Model trained on characters

The code for sampling the generator trained on characters is similar to the code used to sample the generator trained on words. We first load the model, create a z vector, get the Softmax output from the generator, and sample it by taking the mode of the distribution, that is, by sampling the index with the highest probability and converting it into a character using our token_to_id function:

```
import numpy as np
from utils import load_model, sample
```

```
def inference(model_path, weights_path):
    G = load_model(model_path, weights_path)
    z = np.random.uniform(-1, 1, 1)
    res = G.inference(z)
    text = sample(res)
    print(text)
```

In the following table, we provide two examples of a few short sentences generated with the same fixed z vector by a generator at the 340,000 and 356,000 iterations. Despite the fact that the model is not always efficient in producing words and is rarely able to produce valid sequences of words, it is interesting to observe the evolution of the model as it is being trained.

For example, on the first row, the word short was replaced with white, while on the eighth row, haeg and ane were fixed to become hang and are:

340,000 Iterations	356,000 Iterations
'short for was '	'white not was '
'the nhen ends fo'	'the tost bays go'
'report cave glag'	'report lake khou'
'ag the patt conv'	'u manikago prev.'
'mbl a led gold i'	' b i has show i '
'sullo kibute was'	'happi levidy was'
'these aod finnee'	'these and fev re'
'he haeg ane ron '	'he hang are his '
"the soles 's p"	'tne upel was'
'pir the that phite'	'wom there is bounh'

Summary

In this chapter, we explored the use of GANs in the context of discrete time-series prediction. We learned how to implement a model for a generator of discrete sequences with a short vocabulary based on the Adversarial Generation of Natural Language paper by Rajeswar et al. We implemented the models and trained them on sequences of words and sequences of characters.

In the next chapter, we will learn how to perform text-to-image synthesis with GANs.

9
Text-to-Image Synthesis with GANs

In this chapter, you will learn how to implement Generative Adversarial Text-to-image Synthesis, which is a model that generates plausible images from detailed text descriptions. You will learn about the matching-aware discriminator, manifold interpolation, and how to invert the generator for style transfer.

The following topics will be covered in this chapter:

- Text-to-image Synthesis
- Experimental setup
- Model implementation
- Improving the baseline model
- Inference

Technical Requirements

In this chapter, we will focus on the Oxford-102 Flowers dataset that can be downloaded from `http://www.robots.ox.ac.uk/~vgg/data/flowers/102/`.

We will rely on the software libraries included in our Docker container, which are available at `https://github.com/rafaelvalle/hands_on_gans_with_keras/blob/master/Dockerfile`.

You can visit this book's GitHub repo for the full code files: `https://github.com/PacktPublishing/Hands-On-Generative-Adversarial-Networks-with-Keras`.

Text-to-image synthesis

Text-to-image synthesis consists of synthesizing an image that satisfies specifications described in a text sentence. Text-to-image synthesis can be interpreted as a translation problem where the domain of the source and the target are not the same.

In this approach, the problem of text-to-image synthesis is tackled by solving two sub-problems. The first relates to learning a representation of text that encodes the visual specifications described with the text, and the second learning a model that is capable of using the text representation learned to synthesize images that satisfy the specifications described in the text.

For example, consider this text description: *the petals on this flower are white with a yellow center.*

Although broad and not defining many aspects of the target flower, this description provides a few hard specifications about the flower:

- The petals are white
- The center is yellow

In early computer vision, this type of representation would be encoded in hand-engineered attribute representations (Farhadi et al. 2009; Kumar et al. 2009). These attribute representations were normally used to enable zero-shot visual recognition (Fu et al. 2014, Akata et al 2015) and conditional image generation (Yan et al. 2015).

Like most hand-engineered approaches, describing attribute representations by hand is cumbersome and requires domain-specific knowledge. Fortunately, it is possible to learn a vector representation of a text description of an image, thus allowing us to easily manipulate the vector representation of the image by simply modifying the text.

Lately, neural networks have been used to obtain vector representations from words and characters in an unsupervised manner. A related approach has been used to learn discriminative and generalizable text representations for images, as in the work of Reed et al. 2016.

There's an excellent body of work on generative models for image synthesis.

The text-to-image approach combines the work of natural language processing with the work of generative models for image synthesis to produce images based on a text description.

Conditional GANs have been investigated before in the work of Denton et al. (2016), in which the authors explored image synthesis conditioned on class labels instead of text descriptions. Radford et al. (2016) were able to achieve impressive results using vector arithmetic. Nonetheless, as the authors of the paper Generative Adversarial Text -to-image Synthesis mention their paper is the first end-to-end differentiable architecture from the character level to pixel level.

The following image from the paper *Generative Adversarial Text-to-image Synthesis* shows the efficiency of their baseline and improved models regarding image synthesis conditioned on text:

Source: Generative Adversarial Text-to-image Synthesis (https://arxiv.org/abs/1605.05396)

Experimental setup

In this section, we are going to describe and implement functions for loading data, training the models, and logging our experiments.

Data utils

We are going to use the Oxford-102 Flowers dataset along with five text descriptions per image. In this implementation, we are going to use embedding provided by the authors in the paper *Generative Adversarial Text- to-image Synthesis*. You can use text embedding-model, or train a new text-embedding model by following the instructions in the author's GitHub repo: https://github.com/reedscot/icml2016.

We define a helper function to convert images from bytes:

```
def images_from_bytes(byte_images, img_size=(64, 64)):
    # uses PIL's Image to open and resize bytes images using int type
    images = [
        np.array(Image.open(io.BytesIO(img)).resize(img_size), dtype=int)
        for img in byte_images]

    # scales the images to [-1, 1] and cast them to float
    images = np.array(images)
    images = 2 * (images / 255.0) - 1
    images = images.astype(float)
    return images
```

We define a function to iterate over mini-batches of `data` for training:

```
def iterate_minibatches(data, batch_size=128):
    i = 0
    n_samples = len(data[0])
    while True:
        # drop last sample if does not have enough samples
        if len(data) - i*batch_size < batch_size or i == 0:
            ids = np.random.randint(0, n_samples, n_samples)
            np.random.shuffle(ids)
            i = 0

        # load images and their respective embeddings and text
        imgs = data[0][ids[i*batch_size:(i+1)*batch_size]]
        embs = data[1][ids[i*batch_size:(i+1)*batch_size]]
        txts = data[2][ids[i*batch_size:(i+1)*batch_size]]

        # update the batch iterator and yield the data
        i = (i + 1) % len(data)
        yield [imgs, embs, txts]
```

We define a function to load the data:

```
def get_data(filepath, split):
    print("Loading data")
    data_hdfs = h5py.File(filepath, 'r')[split]
    imgs, embs, txtx = [], [], []
    # iterate over hdfs keys to get images, embeddings and texts
    for k in data_hdfs.keys():
        imgs.append(bytes(np.array(data_hdfs[k]['img'])))
        embs.append(np.array(data_hdfs[k]['embeddings']))
        txts.append(np.array(data_hdfs[k]['txt']))
    return [np.array(imgs), np.array(embs), np.array(txts)]
```

Logging utils

We define a function to log text:

```
def log_text(texts, name, i, logger):
    # convert each text to string
    texts = [str(t) for t in texts]
    # use a plus sign and new line to mark a new sentence
    texts = ' +\n'.join(texts)
    # add them to the logger
    logger.add_text('{}'.format(name, i), texts, i)
```

We define a function to log `images` in a 4 x 4 grid:

```
def log_images(images, name, i, logger):
    images = (images.reshape(4, 4, 64, 64, 3)
                    .transpose(0, 2, 1, 3, 4)
                    .reshape(4*64, 4*64, 3))
    images = ((images + 1) * 0.5)
    logger.add_image('{}'.format(name, i), images, i, dataformats='HWC')
```

Training

Our training method is divided into two parts; let's take a look at the function signature first:

```
def train(data_filepath='data/flowers.hdf5', ndf=64, ngf=128, z_dim=128,
          emb_dim=128, lr_d=2e-4, lr_g=2e-4, n_iterations=int(1e6),
          batch_size=64, iters_per_checkpoint=500, n_checkpoint_samples=16,
          out_dir='gan'):
```

Let's look at each argument of our `train` method:

Argument	Description
`data_filepath`	File path to the dataset
`ndf`, `ngf`	Number of discriminator and generator filters
`z_dim`, `emb_dim`	Dimensionality of the noise vector and the text-embedding projection
`lr_d`, `lr_g`	Learning rate of the discriminator and generator
`n_iterations`, `batch_size`, `iters_per_checkpoint`	Self-descriptive
`n_checkpoint_samples`	Samples to log on each checkpoint
`out_dir`	Path to directory where output will be saved

Initial setup

The initial setup for training can be done using the following steps:

1. Add a summary writer for logging using the following code:

```
# add a summary writer for logging
logger = SummaryWriter(out_dir)
logger.add_scalar('d_lr', lr_d, 0)
logger.add_scalar('g_lr', lr_g, 0)
```

2. Load training and validation data and instantiate data iterators:

```
# load training and validation data and instantiate data
iterators
train_data = get_data(data_filepath, 'train')
val_data = get_data(data_filepath, 'valid')
data_iterator = iterate_minibatches(train_data, batch_size)
val_data_iterator = iterate_minibatches(val_data,
n_checkpoint_samples)
```

3. Load the sample validation data to use as a reference during training:

```
# sample validation data to use as reference during training
val_data = next(val_data_iterator)
img_fixed = images_from_bytes(val_data[0])
emb_fixed = val_data[1]
txt_fixed = val_data[2]
```

4. Collect and print image shapes for sanity-checking and building models:

```
img_shape = img_fixed[0].shape
emb_shape = emb_fixed[0].shape
print("emb shape {}".format(img_shape))
print("img shape {}".format(emb_shape))
z_shape = (z_dim, )
```

5. Plot the `real` text for reference:

```
log_images(img_fixed, 'real', '0', logger)
log_text(txt_fixed, 'real', '0', logger)
```

6. Build models using the following code:

```
D = build_discriminator(img_shape, emb_shape, emb_dim, ndf,
                        activation='sigmoid')
G = build_generator(z_shape, emb_shape, emb_dim, ngf)
```

7. Build symbolic model inputs and outputs:

```
real_inputs = Input(shape=img_shape)
txt_inputs = Input(shape=emb_shape)
z_inputs = Input(shape=(z_dim, ))

fake_samples = G([z_inputs, txt_inputs])
D_real = D([real_inputs, txt_inputs])
D_fake = D([fake_samples, txt_inputs])
```

8. Define the D graph and `optimizer` using the following code:

```
G.trainable = False
D.trainable = True
D_model = Model(inputs=[real_inputs, txt_inputs, z_inputs],
                outputs=[D_real, D_fake])
D_model.compile(optimizer=Adam(lr_d, beta_1=0.5, beta_2=0.9),
                loss='binary_crossentropy')
```

9. Define the D(G(z)) graph and optimizer:

```
G.trainable = True
D.trainable = False
G_model = Model(inputs=[z_inputs, txt_inputs], outputs=D_fake)
G_model.compile(Adam(lr=lr_g, beta_1=0.5, beta_2=0.9),
                loss='binary_crossentropy')

ones = np.ones((batch_size, 1, 1, 1), dtype=np.float32)
zeros = np.zeros((batch_size, 1, 1, 1), dtype=np.float32)
```

10. Fix a z vector for the training evaluation:

```
z_fixed = np.random.uniform(-1, 1, size=(n_checkpoint_samples,
z_dim))
```

The initial setup for training is very similar to other GAN setups. As a reference, we include the fixed input to evaluate our generator's progress.

The training loop

Finally, let's look at the training loop in the following steps:

1. Freeze the generator weights and the sample z using the following code:

```
for i in range(n_iterations):
    # freeze generator weights and sample z
    D.trainable = True
    G.trainable = False
    z = np.random.normal(0, 1, size=(batch_size, z_dim))
```

2. Load the training data with images and embedded text:

```
real_batch = next(data_iterator)
images_batch = images_from_bytes(real_batch[0])
emb_text_batch = real_batch[1]
```

3. Compute the discriminator's loss:

```
loss_d = D_model.train_on_batch(
    [images_batch, emb_text_batch, z],
    [ones, zeros, zeros])
```

4. Freeze the discriminator weights and sample z :

```
D.trainable = False
G.trainable = True
z = np.random.normal(0, 1, size=(batch_size, z_dim))
```

5. Load text embeddings and compute the generator's loss:

```
real_batch = next(data_iterator)
loss_g = G_model.train_on_batch([z, real_batch[1]], ones)
```

6. Add fake images to the log and save the model:

```
if (i % iters_per_checkpoint) == 0:
    G.trainable = False
    fake_image = G.predict([z_fixed, emb_fixed])
    log_images(fake_image, 'val_fake', i, logger)
    save_model(G, 'gan')
```

7. Add the losses to the `logger`:

```
log_losses(loss_d, loss_g, i, logger)
```

Model implementation

Our Discriminator and Generator implementations are inspired by the authors' torch implementation: `https://github.com/reedscot/icml2016/blob/master/main_cls.lua`.

Let's start by implementing the wrappers. We assume that the necessary imports are already in place.

Wrapper

We add a wrapper that combines a 2D Convolution with Batchnorm and an optional ReLU. This sequence of layers is very common in this model. In using this wrapper, the code becomes more compact and easier to read:

```
def ConvBatchnormRelu(x, n_filters, kernel_size, strides, padding,
relu=True):
    x = Conv2D(n_filters, kernel_size=kernel_size, strides=strides,
               padding=padding, kernel_initializer=w_init)(x)
    x = BatchNormalization(gamma_initializer=g_init)(x)
    if relu:
        x = Activation('relu')(x)
    return x
```

Let's take a look at the diagram provided by the authors before we implement the **Discriminator** and the **Generator**:

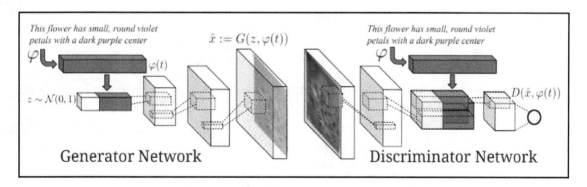

Source: Generative Adversarial Text to Image Synthesis (`https://arxiv.org/abs/1605.05396`)

Discriminator

The Discriminator architecture used in this experiment is very similar to DCGAN. The most important aspects of this implementation are the dense layer on the text embedding and its concatenation with a projection of the image input that goes through multiple 2D Convolutions with Batchnorm and LeakyReLU. This concatenation will go through a couple more Convolutions and produce the final output of the model, which will have a Sigmoid non-linearity, indicating that we are working with the standard GAN framework. We define input for the images and text embeddings using the following code:

```
def build_discriminator(image_input_shape=(64, 64, 3),
text_input_shape=(1024,),
                        embedding_dim=128, ndf=64,
activation='linear'):
    # define inputs for the images and the text embeddings
    image_inputs = Input(shape=image_input_shape,
name='image_input')
    text_inputs = Input(shape=text_input_shape, name='text_input')
```

We do the text embedding on the frontend; we embed the text with a dense layer and leaky relu:

```
    text_embedded = Dense(embedding_dim,
input_shape=text_input_shape,
                          use_bias=True,
kernel_initializer=w_init)(text_inputs)
    text_embedded = LeakyReLU(0.2)(text_embedded)
```

Repeat the text embedding 16 times to create a 4 x 4 by `embedding_dim` tensor:

```
    text_embedded = RepeatVector(16)(text_embedded)
    text_embedded = Reshape((4, 4, embedding_dim))(text_embedded)
```

Then, we do the image embedding on the frontend: sequence of convs with batchnorm and leaky ReLU:

```
    x = Conv2D(ndf, kernel_size=4, strides=2, padding='same',
               kernel_initializer=w_init,
input_shape=image_input_shape)(image_inputs)
    x = LeakyReLU(0.2)(x)
    x = Conv2D(ndf*2, kernel_size=4, strides=2, padding='same',
               kernel_initializer=w_init)(x)
    x = BatchNormalization()(x)
    x = LeakyReLU(0.2)(x)
    x = Conv2D(ndf*4, kernel_size=4, strides=2, padding='same',
               kernel_initializer=w_init)(x)
    x = BatchNormalization()(x)
```

```
x = LeakyReLU(0.2)(x)
x = Conv2D(ndf*8, kernel_size=4, strides=2, padding='same',
           kernel_initializer=w_init)(x)
x = BatchNormalization()(x)
image_embedded = LeakyReLU(0.2)(x)
```

`Concatenate` the embedded text and image using the following code:

```
x = Concatenate()([text_embedded, image_embedded])
```

Use the concatenated embedded text and image to predict the output:

```
x = Conv2D(ndf*8, kernel_size=1, strides=1, padding='valid',
           kernel_initializer=w_init)(x)
x = BatchNormalization()(x)
x = LeakyReLU(0.2)(x)
x = Conv2D(1, kernel_size=4, strides=1, padding='valid',
           kernel_initializer=w_init)(x)
x = Activation(activation)(x)
print("\nDiscriminator")
```

Compile the `model` graph using the following code:

```
model = Model(inputs=[image_inputs, text_inputs], outputs=x,
              name='Discriminator')
model.summary()
return model
```

Generator

In this implementation, the Generator uses multiple residual connections that added the input of a sequence of layers to the output of that sequence of layers. Each sequence of layers consists of a 2D Convolution followed by a Batchnorm and ReLU. The residual connection is then followed by a 2D Transposed Convolution and the operation repeats a few times. First, we define the input using the following code:

```
def build_generator(z_input_shape=(128,), text_input_shape=(1024,),
                     embedding_dim=128, ngf=64, n_channels=3):
    # define inputs
    z_inputs = Input(shape=z_input_shape, name='z_input')
    text_inputs = Input(shape=text_input_shape, name='text_input')
```

Then, we project text embeddings using the following code:

```
text_embedded = Dense(embedding_dim,
input_shape=text_input_shape,
                          use_bias=True,
kernel_initializer=w_init)(text_inputs)
    text_embedded = LeakyReLU(0.2)(text_embedded)
```

Concatenate `text_embedded` and `z` and reshape them using the following code:

```
x = Concatenate()([text_embedded, z_inputs])
x = Reshape((1, 1, embedding_dim+z_input_shape[0]))(x)
x = Conv2DTranspose(ngf*8, kernel_size=4, strides=1,
padding='valid',
                          use_bias=False,
kernel_initializer=w_init)(x)
    h0 = BatchNormalization(gamma_initializer=g_init)(x)
```

Repeatedly project `text_embedded` and `z` with residual connections using stacks of convolutions:

```
x = ConvBatchnormRelu(h0, ngf*2, 1, 1, 'same')
x = ConvBatchnormRelu(x, ngf*2, 3, 1, 'same')
x = ConvBatchnormRelu(x, ngf*8, 3, 1, 'same', relu=False)
x = Activation('relu')(Add()([h0, x]))

x = Conv2DTranspose(ngf*4, kernel_size=4, strides=2,
padding='same',
                          use_bias=False,
kernel_initializer=w_init)(x)
    h1 = BatchNormalization(gamma_initializer=g_init)(x)

x = ConvBatchnormRelu(h1, ngf, 1, 1, 'same')
x = ConvBatchnormRelu(x, ngf, 3, 1, 'same')
x = ConvBatchnormRelu(x, ngf*4, 3, 1, 'same', relu=False)
x = Activation('relu')(Add()([h1, x]))

x = Conv2DTranspose(ngf*2, kernel_size=4, strides=2,
padding='same',
                          use_bias=False,
kernel_initializer=w_init)(x)
    x = BatchNormalization(gamma_initializer=g_init)(x)
    x = Activation('relu')(x)

x = Conv2DTranspose(ngf, kernel_size=4, strides=2,
padding='same',
                          use_bias=False,
kernel_initializer=w_init)(x)
```

```
        x = BatchNormalization(gamma_initializer=g_init)(x)

        x = Conv2DTranspose(n_channels, kernel_size=4, strides=2,
    padding='same',
                            use_bias=False,
    kernel_initializer=w_init)(x)
        x = Activation('tanh')(x)
```

Create the `model` graph using the following code:

```
        model = Model(inputs=[z_inputs, text_inputs], outputs=x,
    name='Generator')
        print("\nGenerator ResNet")
        model.summary()
        return model
```

Improving the baseline model

In this example, we improve the baseline model without doing any modifications to the architecture. The authors propose changing the optimization problem such that the Discriminator also has access to mismatched pairs of text embeddings and images.

This approach is called the Matching-Aware Discriminator and is designed to separate the error sources in this task. During training, the discriminator has access to real images with proper text and synthetic images with arbitrary text. In this context, the discriminator implicitly has two sources of error: fake images that look real but do not match the text description, and unrealistic images for any text.

In this context, the authors explicitly provide the discriminator with pairs of real images and unmatched texts, and empirically find that this helps during training. We'll provide a slice of the training loop with the necessary modifications to perform the Matching-aware approach.

Training

To train the model, we use the following steps:

1. Build the model output, including a variable for the shuffled input:

```
    real_inputs = Input(shape=img_shape)
    txt_inputs = Input(shape=emb_shape)
    txt_shuf_inputs = Input(shape=emb_shape)
    z_inputs = Input(shape=(z_dim, ))
```

2. Instantiate symbolic variables for the discriminator's output:

```
fake_samples = G([z_inputs, txt_inputs])
D_real = D([real_inputs, txt_inputs])
D_wrong = D([real_inputs, txt_shuf_inputs])
D_fake = D([fake_samples, txt_inputs])
```

3. Define the D graph and optimizer, including the shuffled text input:

```
G.trainable = False
D.trainable = True
D_model = Model(inputs=[real_inputs, txt_inputs, txt_shuf_inputs,
z_inputs],
                outputs=[D_real, D_wrong, D_fake])
```

4. Get the data for the images and text embeddings:

```
for i in range(n_iterations):
    # freeze generators weights and sample z
    D.trainable = True
    G.trainable = False
    z = np.random.normal(0, 1, size=(batch_size, z_dim))
    real_batch = next(data_iterator)
    images_batch = images_from_bytes(real_batch[0])
    emb_text_batch = real_batch[1]
```

5. Randomly sample the text embeddings:

```
ids = np.arange(len(emb_text_batch))
np.random.shuffle(ids)
emb_text_batch_shuffle = emb_text_batch[ids]
```

6. Compute the discriminator's loss:

```
loss_d = D_model.train_on_batch(
    [images_batch, emb_text_batch, emb_text_batch_shuffle, z],
    [ones, zeros, zeros])
```

Inference

The imports are shared among all inference experiments:

```
import matplotlib
matplotlib.use("Agg")
import matplotlib.pylab as plt
import numpy as np
from utils import get_data, iterate_minibatches, load_model
```

In the following subsections, we are going to sample our generator in four different manners. We are going to leverage the validation set to collect text embeddings.

Sampling the generator

We randomly sample the generator to informally evaluate image quality with respect to the constraints described in the text. Inference is straightforward and is described in the following code block:

```
def infer(data_filepath='data/flowers.hdf5', z_dim=128, out_dir='gan',
          n_samples=5):
    # we load the saved model
    G = load_model(out_dir)

    # get text embeddings and text from the validation set
    val_data = get_data(data_filepath, 'train')
    val_data = next(iterate_minibatches(val_data, n_samples))
    emb, txts = val_data[1], val_data[2]

    # we sample a z to produce fake images with the text embeddings
    z = np.random.uniform(-1, 1, size=(n_samples, z_dim))
    G.trainable = False
    fake_images = G.predict([z, emb])

    # generate n_samples
    for i in range(n_samples):
        # scale the image to [0, 1]
        img = ((fake_images[i] + 1)*0.5)
        # save image to disk and add text to text file.
        plt.imsave("{}/fake_{}".format(out_dir, i), img)
        print(i, str(txts[i]).strip(),
            file=open("{}/fake_text.txt".format(out_dir), "a"))
```

The following images in the table were synthesized by a generator that uses the text embeddings that correspond to each line of text:

0 this flower has six yellow petals with orange spots and orange edges.	
1 this flower has petals that are purple with white stamen.	
2 these dark yellow flowers grow together in a bunch and have white stamen.	
3 this purple flower has a very large stamen and squiggly, long, thin petals.	
4 this flower has petals that are white with green stamen.	

Interpolation in the Latent Space

We continue our experiments by performing linear interpolation in latent space. We do this by sampling two Z vectors, which are represented as points in a multidimensional space. We interpolate between then by linearly going from one point to another in steps. Let's take a look at the code for doing so:

```
def infer(data_filepath='data/flowers.hdf5',
          z_dim=128, out_dir='gan', n_steps=10):
    # load the saved model
    G = load_model(out_dir)

    # get text embeddings and text from the validation set
    val_data = get_data(data_filepath, 'train')
    val_data = next(iterate_minibatches(val_data, 1))
    emb_fixed, txt_fixed = val_data[1], val_data[2]

    # sample two z vectors to mark our starting and ending z
    z_start = np.random.uniform(-1, 1, size=(1, z_dim))
    z_end = np.random.uniform(-1, 1, size=(1, z_dim))
    G.trainable = False

    # we synthesize n_steps between the source and target z
```

```
for i in range(n_steps+1):
    # define how many steps we have taken with respect to the total
number of steps
    p = i/float(n_steps)
    # linearly interpolate between the start and ending z vectors
    z = z_start * (1-p) + z_end * p

    # sample the generator with the interpolated z vector
    fake_image = G.predict([z, emb_fixed])[0]

    # scale and save the generated image. save the corresponding text
    img = ((fake_image + 1)*0.5)
    plt.imsave("{}/fake_z_interpolation_i{}".format(out_dir, i), img)
    print(i, str(txt_fixed[0]).strip(),
        file=open("{}/fake_z_interpolation.txt".format(out_dir),
"a"))
```

The following images were generated by interpolating the latent space and using this fixed phrase:

this flower has pink and white petals with some being sure white petals and yellow stamen

Interestingly, generating images with interpolation space produces images that are very similar if not the same. This behavior is common in GAN models in which the Generator has access to an input that is sufficient to predict the output, resulting in the generator ignoring the latent vector, Z. We forward readers interested in understanding this problem to the paper *Unpaired Image-to-Image Translation using Cycle-Consistent Adversarial Networks* written by Jun-Yan Zhu et al. from UC Berkeley:

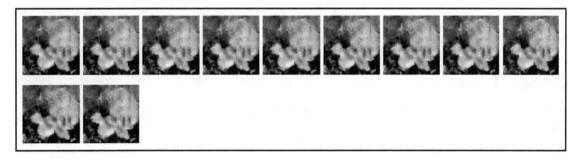

Interpolation in Latent Space

Interpolation in the text-embedding space

These experiments perform linear interpolation in the text-embedding space. In a similar way to the previous experiment, we do this by sampling two text-embedding vectors, which are represented as points in a multidimensional space. We interpolate between them by linearly going from one point to another in N steps.

The following code block is used for inference with interpolation in the text-embedding space:

```
def infer(data_filepath='data/flowers.hdf5', z_dim=128, out_dir='gan',
          n_steps=10):
    # we load the saved model
    G = load_model(out_dir)
    # get text embeddings and text from the validation set
    val_data = get_data(data_filepath, 'train')
    val_data = next(iterate_minibatches(val_data, 2))
    # sample to text embeddings to represent the starting and ending points
    emb_source, emb_target = val_data[1]
    txts = val_data[2]
    z = np.random.uniform(-1, 1, size=(1, z_dim))
    G.trainable = False

    # synthesize n_steps from source to target
    for i in range(n_steps+1):
        # define how many steps we have taken with respect to the total
number of steps
        p = i/float(n_steps)

        # linearly interpolate between embeddings
        emb = emb_source * (1-p) + emb_target * p
        emb = emb[None, :]

        # samples the generator
        fake_image = G.predict([z, emb])[0]
```

Plot and scale the image to [0, 1] and save the corresponding text using the following code:

```
        img = ((fake_image + 1)*0.5)
        plt.imsave("{}/fake_text_interpolation_i{}".format(out_dir, i),
img)
        print(i, str(txts[int(round(p))]).strip(),
            file=open("{}/fake_text_interpolation.txt".format(out_dir),
"a"))
```

The upcoming images were generated by interpolating in the text-embedding space and using a fixed Z. Notice that by interpolating between the text-embedding vectors, we are able to gradually transition from one image to another. This is a fascinating characteristic of generative models that takes advantage of such embeddings and suggests that we can perform arithmetic in the embedding space as well:

TEXT EMBEDDING INTERPOLATION	TEXT	IMAGE
10/10 0/10	this flower is vibrant red in color with a single style that is multi-colored. this flower has yellow and orange petals with a dark spot at the base of each petal.	
9/10 1/10	this flower is vibrant red in color with a single style that is multi-colored. this flower has yellow and orange petals with a dark spot at the base of each petal.	
8/10 2/10	this flower is vibrant red in color with a single style that is multi-colored. this flower has yellow and orange petals with a dark spot at the base of each petal.	
7/10 3/10	this flower is vibrant red in color with a single style that is multi-colored. this flower has yellow and orange petals with a dark spot at the base of each petal.	
6/10 4/10	this flower is vibrant red in color with a single style that is multi-colored. this flower has yellow and orange petals with a dark spot at the base of each petal.	
5/10 5/10	this flower is vibrant red in color with a single style that is multi-colored. this flower has yellow and orange petals with a dark spot at the base of each petal.	
4/10 6/10	this flower is vibrant red in color with a single style that is multi-colored. this flower has yellow and orange petals with a dark spot at the base of each petal.	
3/10 7/10	this flower is vibrant red in color with a single style that is multi-colored. this flower has yellow and orange petals with a dark spot at the base of each petal.	

2/10 8/10	this flower is vibrant red in color with a single style that is multi-colored. this flower has yellow and orange petals with a dark spot at the base of each petal.	
1/10 9/10	this flower is vibrant red in color with a single style that is multi-colored. this flower has yellow and orange petals with a dark spot at the base of each petal.	
9/10 10/10	this flower is vibrant red in color with a single style that is multi-colored. this flower has yellow and orange petals with a dark spot at the base of each petal.	

Interpolation in the text-embedding space

Inferencing with arithmetic in the text-embedding space

Arithmetic in the embedding space is another fascinating aspect of some generative models. In vector arithmetic in embedding spaces, the elementary mathematical operations, such as add or subtract, are closely related to adding properties described in two vectors or subtracting a property described in one vector from the other. For example, adding text vectors that describe orange and yellow flowers, respectively, can result in flowers that have both colors.

The following code block was used to perform vector arithmetic in the text-embedding space:

```
def infer(data_filepath='data/flowers.hdf5', z_dim=128, out_dir='gan',
        n_steps=10):
    # load the saved model
    G = load_model(out_dir)

    # load embeddings and text from the validation dataset
    val_data = get_data(data_filepath, 'train')
    val_data = next(iterate_minibatches(val_data, 2))
    emb_a, emb_b = val_data[1]
    txts = val_data[2]
    # add batch dimension
    emb_a, emb_b = emb_a[None, :], emb_b[None, :]
    # sample z vector for inference
    z = np.random.uniform(-1, 1, size=(1, z_dim))
```

```
G.trainable = False
# predict two images using embeddings a and b
fake_image_a = G.predict([z, emb_a])[0]
fake_image_b = G.predict([z, emb_b])[0]

# add and subtract the embeddings
emb_add = (emb_a + emb_b)
emb_a_sub_b = (emb_a - emb_b)
emb_b_sub_a = (emb_b - emb_a)
```

Generate images with the added and subtracted embeddings using the following code:

```
fake_a = G.predict([z, emb_a])[0]
fake_b = G.predict([z, emb_b])[0]
fake_add = G.predict([z, emb_add])[0]
fake_a_sub_b = G.predict([z, emb_a_sub_b])[0]
fake_b_sub_a = G.predict([z, emb_b_sub_a])[0]
# scale fake images to [0, 1]
fake_a = ((fake_a + 1)*0.5)
fake_b = ((fake_b + 1)*0.5)
fake_add = ((fake_add + 1)*0.5)
fake_a_sub_b = ((fake_a_sub_b + 1)*0.5)
fake_b_sub_a = ((fake_b_sub_a + 1)*0.5)
# plot the images and save text to disk
plt.imsave("{}/fake_text_arithmetic_a".format(out_dir), fake_a)
plt.imsave("{}/fake_text_arithmetic_b".format(out_dir), fake_b)
plt.imsave("{}/fake_text_arithmetic_add".format(out_dir), fake_add)
plt.imsave("{}/fake_text_arithmetic_a_sub_b".format(out_dir),
fake_a_sub_b)
plt.imsave("{}/fake_text_arithmetic_b_sub_a".format(out_dir),
fake_b_sub_a)
print(str(txts[0]), str(txts[1]),
        file=open("{}/fake_text_arithmetic.txt".format(out_dir), "a"))
```

In the following image, fake sample A is a yellow flower and fake sample B is an orange flower. Not surprisingly, by adding their respective text embeddings together, we are able to synthesize a flower that combines the properties in A and B:

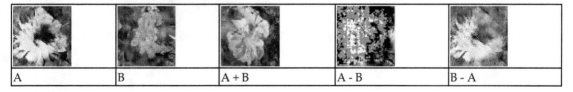

| A | B | A + B | A - B | B - A |

 In this case subtracting embedding does not produce interesting results.

Summary

In this chapter, you learned how to implement the Discriminator and Generator described in the paper *Generative Adversarial Text to Image Synthesis*. You learned how to implement the baseline trained on the Oxford-102 Flowers dataset. You also learned how to improve the baseline by using the matching-aware discriminator. Finally, you learned how to perform multiple types of inference using random sampling and interpolation in Z space, interpolation on the text-embedding space, and arithmetic on the text-embedding space.

In the next chapter, we will learn about speech enhancement with GANs.

10
Speech Enhancement with GANs

In this chapter, you will learn how to implement a **Speech Enhancement Generative Adversarial Network (SEGAN)**, a framework for audio denoising and speech enhancement using GANs, developed by Santiago Pascual and others. You will learn to train the model on multiple speakers and noise conditions. You will learn to evaluate the model qualitatively and quantitatively. By the end of the chapter, you will have learned to train and have a model for speech enhancement.

At the end of this chapter, you will be able to implement your own speech enhancement model and evaluate its performance.

The following topics will be covered in this chapter:

- Audio enhancement
- Experimental setup
- Model implementation: SEGAN
- Qualitative and quantitative evaluation

Technical requirements

In this chapter, we will focus on the WSJ dataset and a noise dataset that can be downloaded from `https://datashare.is.ed.ac.uk/handle/10283/1942`.

If you prefer, you can use the script provided on the SEGAN GitHub page: `https://github.com/santi-pdp/segan/blob/master/prepare_data.sh`.

We will rely on the software libraries included in our Docker container available at `https://github.com/packt/hands_on_gans_with_keras/blob/master/Dockerfile`.

You can visit the GitHub repository of this book for the full code files at the following link: `https://github.com/PacktPublishing/Hands-On-Generative-Adversarial-Networks-with-Keras`.

Audio enhancement

Broadly speaking, audio enhancement is an umbrella term that is used by the research community and refers to enhancing the quality of an audio signal. Audio signals are degraded in many forms, be it in the form of interventions from other audio signals or failure in the network that results in lost packets, severe compression, and even material waste associated with the form in which it is stored. Audio enhancement can take forms such as source separation, audio repair, and audio inpainting.

On a daily basis, our ears receive an audio mixture comprised of sounds inside and outside our environment that are able to travel to us. Although our ears receive an audio mixture, we are able to actively ignore other signals and focus on the audio signal that we are interested in. For example, listen carefully to the sounds in your environment that you were not aware of and become aware of how you can focus on one sound at a time.

Machine listening, on the other hand, does not have the explicit ability to separate the target source from the audio mixture. This brings us to one of the first approaches to audio enhancement called **source separation.**

In source separation, the audio signal is assumed to be an audio mixture that is created by adding multiple audio signals together. In this case, we can extract the target audio by subtracting the noise signal from the mixture because the relationship between the target signal and the noise is additive. The following screenshot produced with the iZotope RX illustrates the waveform of a noise signal in 16 kHz:

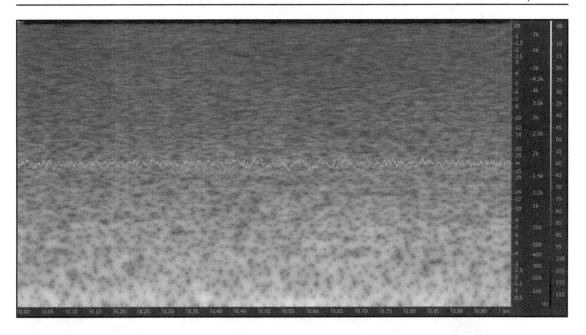

The following screenshot, produced with iZotope RX, illustrates a spectrogram of a target signal in 16 kHz:

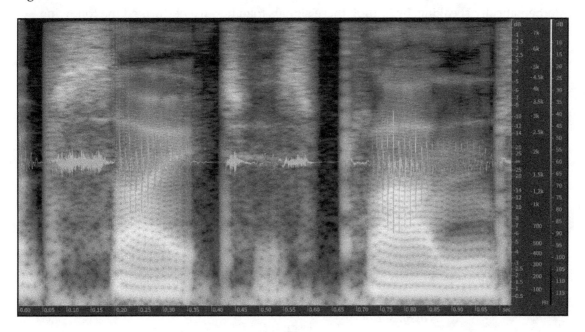

By adding these signals together, we get the following waveform and spectrogram, which is a noisy signal in 16 kHz:

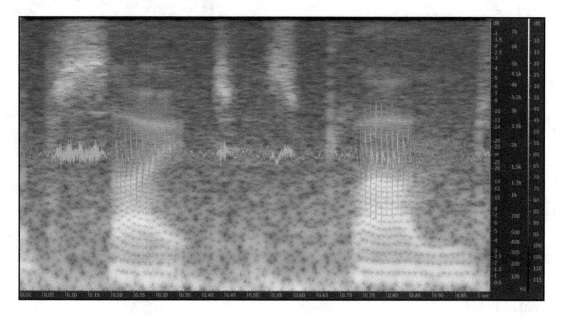

Mathematically speaking, by adding these signals together, we performed the following operation:

$$NoisyAudio[t] = Noise[t] + Target[t]$$,

where *Noisy Audio, Noise,* and *Target* are time series.

As can be seen in the preceding equation, we can extract the target audio from the mixture by subtracting the noise signal from it at every time step [*t*]:

$$Target[t] = NoisyAudio[t] - Noise[t]$$

Note that an additive relationship between *target* and *noise* is just one of many relationships. As a matter of fact, target audio can be damaged in multiple ways.

For example, let's consider clipped audio in which the magnitude of peak values are clipped at 0.9. Mathematically speaking, this is equal to the following:

$$NoisyAudio(x[t]) = \begin{cases} x[t], & \text{if } |x| < 0.9 \\ \operatorname{sgn} x[t] * 0.9, & \text{otherwise} \end{cases}$$

In this case, the relationship between the target audio and the noisy audio is not additive: we need to perform **audio repair** on the damaged signal. If the amount of clipping is minimal, a simple interpolation efficient will be effective.

In the worst cases of damaged audio, a portion of the target audio is completely missing or so damaged that the target audio cannot be extracted. In such extreme cases, audio enhancement becomes audio synthesis or **audio inpainting**. In speech, for example, **audio inpainting** assumes that the audio enhancement model either has a language model or has access to words that it should use to inpaint the missing audio segment.

In this chapter, we are going to focus mainly on audio enhancement in the context of **source separation**.

There are many approaches to speech enhancement. The book *Speech Enhancement* by Philipos C. Loizou divides speech enhancement techniques into four groups, including spectral subtraction, Wiener filtering, statistical model-based methods, and subspace algorithms. In recent years, model-based methods using neural networks have achieved excellent results in speech enhancement. Most of such neural network methods operate on the frequency domain and **Speech Enhancement Generative Adversarial Network (SEGAN)** is one of the first neural network approaches to operate on the time domain.

Experimental setup

In this section, we are going to implement our data loader, our training function, and our loggers.

Data

We are going to use speech enhancement dataset described in the paper *Noisy speech database for training speech enhancement algorithms and TTS models*. As it is described in the SEGAN paper, this dataset uses clean speech data from the Voice Bank corpus, using 28 speakers for the training set and two speakers for the test set. The noise dataset comes from the Demand database. The noisy training set is built by adding 10 types of noise (two artificial and eight from the Demand database) at four signal-to-noise ratios (15, 10, 5, and 0 dB) to the clean speech.

The iterating over minibatches can be divided in three steps as follows:

1. Create a list with all wave files in the clean and noisy data paths by using `glob`:

    ```
    def iterate_minibatches(clean_data_path, noisy_data_path,
    segment_length=16384,
                            batch_size=128):
    clean_filepaths = sorted(glob(clean_data_path+"*.wav"))
    noisy_filepaths = sorted(glob(noisy_data_path+"*.wav"))
    n_files = len(clean_filepaths)
    cur_batch = 0
    ```

2. Randomly sample clean and noisy pairs using `np.random.choice`:

    ```
    while True:
    # first iter or drop last?
    if (n_files - cur_batch*batch_size) < batch_size or cur_batch == 0:
        ids = np.random.choice(range(n_files), n_files, replace=False)
        np.random.shuffle(ids)
        cur_batch = 0

    train_data = []
    for i in range(batch_size):
        sr_clean, clean_data =
    read(clean_filepaths[ids[cur_batch*batch_size+i]])
        sr_noisy, noisy_data =
    read(noisy_filepaths[ids[cur_batch*batch_size+i]])
    ```

3. Randomly sample segment lengths from the randomly selected samples by using `np.random.randint`:

    ```
    # randomly sample segments on each file
    start_id = np.random.randint(0, len(clean_data) -
    segment_length)
    clean_data = clean_data[start_id:start_id+segment_length]
    noisy_data = noisy_data[start_id:start_id+segment_length]
    clean_data = clean_data[None, :, None]
    noisy_data = noisy_data[None, :, None]
    train_data.append([clean_data, noisy_data])
    cur_batch = (cur_batch + 1) %
    int(len(clean_filepaths)/batch_size)

    # scale data to [-1, 1] range
    train_data = np.array(train_data) / MAX_WAV_VALUE
    yield train_data, cur_batch
    ```

Training

Our training method consists of two parts:

- Initializing the required variables and compiling models
- The training loop itself

We will start by looking at the training method's signature:

```
def train(ndf=64, ngf=64, use_upsampling=False, lr_d=5e-5,
lr_g=5e-5,
        reconstruction_weight=100,
    segment_length=16384, n_checkpoint_audio=8,
n_iterations=int(1e6), batch_size=256,
    out_dir='lsgan_segan_transpose'):
```

Let's look at each argument of our `train` method in the following table:

Argument	Description
ndf, ngf	number of discriminator and generator filters
use_upsampling	whether to use upsampling or transposed convolutions
lr_d, lr_g	learning rate of the discriminator and generator
reconstruction_weight	weight of the reconstruction loss
segment_length,	length of the audio file in seconds
n_checkpoint_audio, n_iterations, batch_size	self-descriptive
out_dir	path to directory where outputs will be saved

Initializations

Let's implement the first part of our `train` method. First we instantiate our logger and set it to output logs to `out_dir` and instantiate our data iterator:

```
logger = SummaryWriter(out_dir)
data_iterator = iterate_minibatches(
    CLEAN_DATA_PATH, NOISY_DATA_PATH, segment_length, batch_size)
```

We then define input shapes that will be used to instantiate our generator and discriminator, using the following code:

```
clean_input_shape = (1, 16384, 1)
noisy_input_shape = (1, 16384, 1)
z_input_shape = (1, 16, 1024)
```

Next, we build the Discriminator D and the Generator G, using the following code:

```
D = build_segan_discriminator(noisy_input_shape, clean_input_shape)
G = build_segan_generator(noisy_input_shape, z_input_shape,
use_upsampling=use_upsampling)
```

Using the following code, we define the computational graph for D and the optimizer:

```
D.compile(optimizer=RMSprop(lr_d), loss='mse')
```

The following code block defines the computational graph for $D(G(Z))$, the output for the D discriminator on fake data $G(z)$ produced by the G generator:

```
D.trainable = False
z_input = Input(shape=z_input_shape)
noisy_input = Input(shape=noisy_input_shape)
clean_input = Input(shape=clean_input_shape)
denoised_output = G([noisy_input, z_input])
D_fake = D([noisy_input, denoised_output])
D_of_G = Model(inputs=[noisy_input, z_input, clean_input],
        outputs=[D_fake, denoised_output])
```

Then, we define a custom reconstruction loss function that takes both the clean audio and the denoised audio produced by the generator. The code block looks like this:

```
loss_reconstruction = partial(mean_absolute_error,
        denoised_audio=denoised_output,
        clean_audio=clean_input)
```

Now that the graph is described, we can finally compile $D(G(Z))$:

```
D_of_G.compile(RMSprop(lr=lr_g),
        loss=['mse', loss_reconstruction],
        loss_weights=[1, reconstruction_weight])
```

To define the variables for computing `loss`, we use the following code block:

```
ones = np.ones((batch_size, 1), dtype=np.float32)
zeros = np.zeros((batch_size, 1), dtype=np.float32)
dummy = np.zeros((batch_size, 1), dtype=np.float32)
```

To evaluate the generator's progress during training, we fix a z vector, using the following code block:

```
z_fixed = np.random.normal(0, 1, size=(n_checkpoint_audio,) +
z_input_shape)
```

And we add the following code to log a few examples for reference during training:

```
data_batch, cur_batch = next(data_iterator)
clean_fixed = data_batch[:n_checkpoint_audio, 0]
noisy_fixed = data_batch[:n_checkpoint_audio, 1]
log_audio(clean_fixed[:, 0, :, 0], logger, 'clean')
log_audio(noisy_fixed[:, 0, :, 0], logger, 'noisy')
```

Training loop

Implement the second part of the `train` method using the following steps:

1. Log denoise audio in every epoch:

```
epoch = 0
for i in range(n_iterations):
    # log denoised audio every epoch
    if cur_batch == 1:
        G.trainable = False
        fake_audio = G.predict([noisy_fixed, z_fixed])
        log_audio(fake_audio[:n_checkpoint_audio, 0, :, 0],
logger, 'denoised')
        epoch += 1
```

2. Make the Discriminator `trainable` and freeze the Generator weights

```
D.trainable = True
G.trainable = False
```

3. Sample z and data, and train the discriminator on a single batch:

```
z = np.random.normal(0, 1, size=(batch_size, ) +
z_input_shape)
    data_batch, cur_batch = next(data_iterator)
    clean_batch = data_batch[:, 0]
    noisy_batch = data_batch[:, 1]
    fake_batch = G.predict([noisy_batch, z])
    loss_real = D.train_on_batch([noisy_batch, clean_batch],
ones)
    loss_fake = D.train_on_batch([noisy_batch, fake_batch],
zeros)
    loss_d = [loss_real + loss_fake, loss_real, loss_fake]
```

4. Make the Generator trainable and freeze the Discriminator weights:

```
D.trainable = False
G.trainable = True
```

5. Sample z and data, then train the generator on a single batch:

```
z = np.random.normal(0, 1, size=(batch_size, ) +
z_input_shape)
    data_batch, cur_batch = next(data_iterator)
    clean_batch = data_batch[:, 0]
    noisy_batch = data_batch[:, 1]
    loss_g = D_of_G.train_on_batch([noisy_batch, z,
clean_batch], [ones, dummy])
```

6. Log discriminator and generator loss:

```
log_losses(loss_d, loss_g, i, logger)
```

Logging audio files and losses

For logging, we take advantage of the Tensorboard ability to log audio files by using the routine .add_audio. This function takes as input the name of the tab associated with the audio field, the audio, the iteration number, and the sampling rate.

```
def log_audio(audios, logger, name="synthesis", sr=16000):
    for i in range(len(audios)):
        logger.add_audio('{}_{}'.format(name, i), audios[i], 0,
sample_rate=sr)
```

For reporting losses, we include an extra scalar for the generator's reconstruction loss. The `add_scalar` function takes as input the name of the tab associated with this scalar field, the scalar value and the iteration number:

```
def log_losses(loss_d, loss_g, iteration, logger):
    # define the tag, loss, and iteration to be logged.
    logger.add_scalar("losses_d", loss_d[0], iteration)
    logger.add_scalar("losses_d_real", loss_d[1], iteration)
    logger.add_scalar("losses_d_fake", loss_d[2], iteration)
    logger.add_scalar("losses_g", loss_g[0], iteration)
    logger.add_scalar("losses_g_fake", loss_g[1], iteration)
    logger.add_scalar("losses_g_reconstruction", loss_g[2], iteration)
```

Model implementation: SEGAN

In this section, we are going to implement the Discriminator and the generator proposed in the Speech Enhancement GANs paper. Whereas, the discriminator takes as input a clean and a noisy waveform, the generator takes in a noisy waveform and a z vector and uses them to produce a denoised version of the noisy waveform.

Discriminator

In SEGAN, the discriminator architecture is similar to DCGAN and comprises a series of convolutions with batchnorm and parametric ReLUs followed by a few dense layers. The main advantage of parametric ReLUs over ReLUs and leakyReLUs is that the model and the optimization problem being solved will define the best parameter of the leaky ReLU.

Let's start with the necessary imports:

```
from keras.layers import Input, Reshape
from keras.layers.advanced_activations import PReLU
from keras.layers.convolutional import Conv2D
from keras.layers.core import Dense, Flatten
from keras.layers.normalization import BatchNormalization
from keras.models import Model
```

And proceed with the discriminator implementation itself:

```
def build_segan_discriminator(noisy_input_shape, clean_input_shape,
    n_filters=[64, 128, 256, 512, 1024], kernel_size=(1, 31)):
    clean_input = Input(shape=clean_input_shape)
    noisy_input = Input(shape=noisy_input_shape)
```

```
# concatenate inputs on the channel dimension
x = Concatenate(-1)([clean_input, noisy_input])
# convolution layers
for i in range(len(n_filters)):
    x = Conv2D(filters=n_filters[i], kernel_size=kernel_size,
        strides=(1, 4), padding='same', use_bias=True,
        kernel_initializer=weight_init)(x)
    x = BatchNormalization(epsilon=1e-5, momentum=0.1)(x)
    x = PReLU()(x)
```

Reshape x to match the dense layer number of dimensions required:

```
x = Reshape((16384, ))(x)

# dense layers
x = Dense(256, activation=None, use_bias=True)(x)
x = PReLU()(x)
x = Dense(128, activation=None, use_bias=True)(x)
x = PReLU()(x)

# SEGAN uses Least-Squares GAN, hence the activation is linear
x = Dense(1, activation=None, use_bias=True)(x)
```

And finally, create the model graph, using the following code:

```
model = Model(inputs=[noisy_input, clean_input], outputs=x,
name='Discriminator')
    print("\nDiscriminator")
    model.summary()
    return model
```

Generator

SEGAN's generator uses the U-Net architecture: an auto-encoder architecture with residual connections. The generator's encoder uses a series of convolutions to project the noisy input to a smaller dimension. The generator's decoder uses a stack of transposed convolutions to project from the smaller dimension to the original dimension of the data, in this case, audio. With the exception of the first decoder layer that takes the z vector, every decoder layer takes the previous output and the associated encoder output, the residual connection, as input. In addition, SEGAN uses a scale layer on each residual connection as shown in the following diagram:

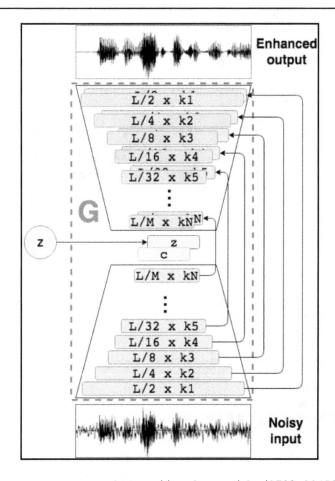

Source: Speech Enhancement GANs(https://arxiv.org/abs/1703.09452)

We will start the generator's implementation by coding the custom ScaleLayer :

```
from keras import backend as K
from keras.layers import Layer
class ScaleLayer(Layer):
    def __init__(self, output_dim, **kwargs):
        self.output_dim = output_dim
        super(ScaleLayer, self).__init__(**kwargs)
    def build(self, input_shape):
        self.weights = self.add_weight(
            name='weights', shape=(input_shape[1], self.output_dim),
            initializer=Ones(), trainable=True)
        super(ScaleLayer, self).build(input_shape)
    def call(self, x):
```

```
        return x * self.weights
    def compute_output_shape(self, input_shape):
        return (input_shape[0], self.output_dim)
```

Now, we are going to implement the generator's architecture. Let's start with the necessary imports to build the model:

```
from keras.layers import Input, Activation, Concatenate, Flatten
from keras.layers import Conv2D, Conv2DTranspose, Dense, UpSampling2D
from keras.layers.advanced_activations import PReLU
from keras.layers.normalization import BatchNormalization
from keras.models import Model
from keras import backend as K
from keras.layers import Layer
```

Now, let's look at the model code:

```
def build_segan_generator(noisy_input_shape, z_input_shape,
                          n_filters=[64, 128, 256, 512, 1024],
                          kernel_size=(1, 31), use_upsampling=False):
    noisy_input = Input(shape=noisy_input_shape)
    z_input = Input(shape=z_input_shape)
```

Create an array to store the skip_connections:

```
    skip_connections = []
```

Then, define the encoder using the following code:

```
    x = noisy_input
    for i in range(len(n_filters)):
        x = Conv2D(filters=n_filters[i], kernel_size=kernel_size,
                   strides=(1, 4), padding='same', use_bias=True,
                   kernel_initializer=weight_init)(x)
        x = PReLU()(x)
        skip_connections.append(ScaleLayer(n_filters[i])(x))
```

Pretend single channel filter and remove the last filter size and update the current x input:

```
    n_filters = [1] + n_filters[:-1]

    # update current x input
    x = z_input
```

Then, define the decoder using the following code:

```
    for i in range(len(n_filters)-1, -1, -1):
        x = Concatenate(3)([x, skip_connections[i]])
        if use_upsampling:
```

```
x = UpSampling2D(size=(1, 4))(x)
x = Conv2D(filters=n_filters[i], kernel_size=kernel_size,
           strides=(1, 1), padding='same',
           kernel_initializer=weight_init, use_bias=True)(x)
    else:
        x = Conv2DTranspose(filters=n_filters[i],
kernel_size=kernel_size,
           strides=(1, 4), padding='same',
           kernel_initializer=weight_init)(x)
    x = PReLU()(x) if i > 0 else Activation("tanh")(x)
```

Finally, create the `model` graph:

```
model = Model(inputs=[noisy_input, z_input], outputs=x,
name='Generator')
    print("\nGenerator")
    model.summary()
    return model
```

Qualitative and quantitative evaluation

In this section, we are going to review and implement qualitative and quantitative methods for audio enhancement techniques.

Qualitative evaluation

As we discussed earlier, qualitative techniques provide a quick way to confirm that training and the models being trained are producing the expected results. In this chapter, we used the Tensorboard ability to include audio files to listen to model outputs during training. The following is a screenshot of the Tensorboard interface showcasing clean, denoised, and noisy audio files:

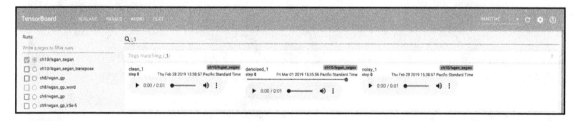

In addition to listening to the audio files, we can look at the spectrograms. The following is an example of a waveform and spectrogram obtained with the iZotope RX from a clean audio signal:

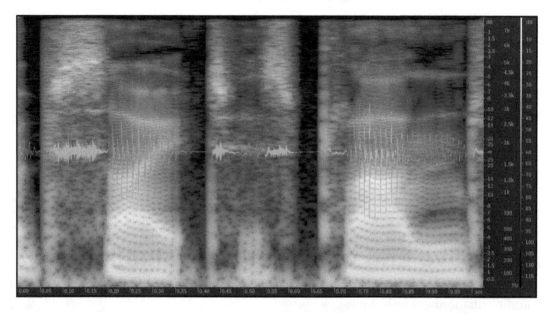

The following is an example of waveform and spectrogram obtained with the iZotope RX from a clean noisy audio signal:

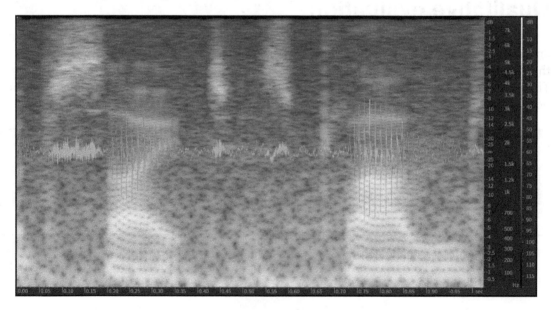

The following is an example of waveform and spectrogram obtained with the iZotope RX from a clean denoised audio signal:

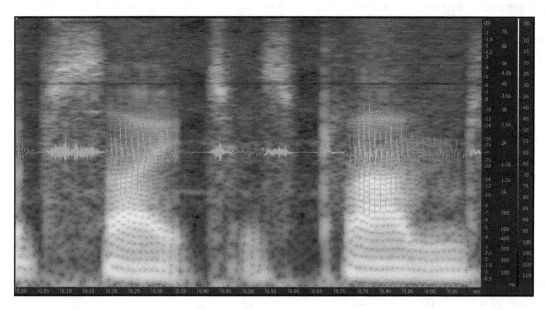

By comparing the noisy and denoised audio to the clean audio, we can quickly confirm that the model that output the denoised audio is cleaning the noisy audio. Notice that in such evaluations it is essential to compare the results to the target audio we want to reproduce, in this case, the clean audio.

Quantitative evaluation

Unlike qualitative techniques that provide a subjective evaluation, quantitative methods are useful because they provide an objective evaluation that is easy to compare against other results.

There are several objective measures of audio quality including **Signal to Noise Ratio (SNR)**, **Segmental Signal to Noise Ratio (SSNR)**, **Perceptual Evaluation of Speech Quality (PESQ)**, **Perception Model-Based Quality (PEM-Q)** estimation, and many others. We will focus on SNR and SSNR.

For a detailed information on speech enhancement and objective measures of speech quality, we recommend the book *Speech Enhancement* by Philipos C. Loizou.

SNR and SSNR

The simplest objective audio quality measure in the time domain is the SNR. The SNR compares two audio signals, sample by sample. It is normally used to measure the speech energy to non-speech energy ratio. Mathematically, SNR is defined as the ratio of the power of the clean signal x to the power of the noise y:

$$SNR(x, y) = 10 \, log_{10} \frac{\sum_{i=1}^{N} x[i]^2}{\sum_{i=1}^{N} y[i]^2)}$$

The implementation in Python is straightforward, and it takes the two audio signals as inputs:

```
def SNR(x, y):
    return 10 * np.log10(np.sum(x**2) / np.sum(y**2))
```

For evaluation the SNR of our model predictions, we need to extract the noise from the model prediction. Assuming that the noise is additive and that the phases of the clean signal x and the denoised signal $\hat{x}$ are aligned, one can obtain the noise by subtracting x from $\hat{x}$ and finally compute the SNR as follows:

$$SNR(x, \hat{x}) = 10 \, log_{10} \frac{\sum_{i=1}^{N} x[i]^2}{\sum_{i=1}^{N} ((x([i] - \hat{x}[i])^2)}$$

Note that this is the only position under the conditions we enumerated. If the phases are not aligned, for example, the difference between the clean signal and the denoised signal will be different and the SNR will change.

As the name describes, SSNR calculates the average of the SNR values of short segments (15 to 20 ms):

$$SSNR = \frac{10}{M} \sum_{m=0}^{M-1} log_{10} \sum_{i=Nm}^{Nm+N-1} \frac{\sum_{i=1}^{N} x[i]^2}{\sum_{i=1}^{N} ((x([i] - y[i])^2)}$$

where N is the segment length and M is the number of segments.

The implementation in Python is straightforward and in addition to the two audio signals, it takes the segment length in seconds as inputs:

```
def SSNR(x, y, segment_length):
    # zero pad to simplify computation
    x = x + [0] * (len(x) % segment_length)
    y = y + [0] * (len(x) % segment_length)
    n_segments = len(x) / segment_length

    ssnr = 0
    for i in range(0, len(x), segment_length):
        ssnr += SNR(x[i:i+segment_length], x[i:i+segment_length])
    return ssnr * 10 / n_segments
```

Summary

In this chapter, we learned about the challenges in audio enhancement, especially in speech, and the advantages of the SEGAN implementation. We learned how to implement the SEGAN model and its loss function that combines the adversarial loss with the L1 reconstruction loss. We also learned how to train the model by writing the training routine and loading the clean and noisy data. Then, we learned how to evaluate the model qualitatively by using Tensorboard and listening to audio samples. We also learned to evaluate the samples qualitatively by comparing spectrograms using the iZotope RX. Finally, we learned how to evaluate the model quantitatively by computing the SNR and the SSNR between the clean data and the denoised data.

In the next chapter, we will learn TequilaGAN: identifying GAM samples.

11
TequilaGAN - Identifying GAN Samples

In this chapter, you will learn how to implement TequilaGAN: How to easily identify GAN samples. You will learn how to understand what the underlying characteristics of **Generative Adversarial Networks (GANs)** data are and how to identify data to differentiate real data from fake data. You will implement strategies to easily identify fake samples generated with the GAN framework. One strategy is based on the statistical analysis and comparison of raw pixel values and features extracted from them. The other strategy learns formal specifications from the real data and shows that fake samples violate the specifications of the real data.

The following topics will be covered in this chapter:

- Identifying GAN samples
- Feature extraction
- Metrics
- Experiments

Technical requirements

In this chapter, we will focus on the MNIST dataset of handwritten images, which can be downloaded from the following link: `http://yann.lecun.com/exdb/mnist/`.

You can download and view the code files in this chapter on the GitHub repository of this book in the following link: `https://github.com/PacktPublishing/Hands-On-Generative-Adversarial-Networks-with-Keras`.

Identifying GAN samples

Fake samples generated with the GANs (Goodfellow et al., 2014) framework have fooled humans and machines into believing that they are indistinguishable from real samples. Although this might be true for the naked eye and the discriminator fooled by the generator, it is unlikely that fake samples are numerically indistinguishable from real samples. Inspired by formal methods, this paper focuses on the evaluation of fake samples with respect to statistical summaries and formal specifications computed on the real data.

Since the *Generative Adversarial Networks* paper (Goodfellow et al., 2014), most GAN-related publications use a grid of image samples to accompany theoretical and empirical results. Unlike **Variational Autoencoders** (**VAEs**) and other models (Goodfellow et al., 2014), most of the evaluation of the output of GAN-trained Generators is qualitative: authors normally list higher sample quality as one of the advantages of their method over other methods. Although numerical measures such as the inception score are used to evaluate GAN samples (Salimans et al., 2016), interestingly, little is mentioned about the numerical properties of fake samples and how these properties compare to real samples.

In the context of Verified Artificial Intelligence (Seshia and Sadigh, 2016), it is hard to systematically verify that the output of a model satisfies the specifications of the data it was trained on, especially when verification depends on the existence of perceptually meaningful features. For example, consider a model that generates images of humans: although it is possible to compare color histograms of real and fake samples, we do not yet have robust algorithms to verify whether an image follows specifications derived from anatomy.

In their very interesting paper *Intriguing Properties of Neural Networks*, Szegedy et al. showed that neural networks can be sensitive to perturbations to an image that are hardly perceptible for humans. The following image is one example of this, where, after applying the perturbation on the middle column on the image on the first column, the network classifies every perturbed image on the third column as an ostrich:

Adversarial examples generated for AlexNet. Source: Intriguing Properties of Neural Networks (https://arxiv.org/abs/1312.6199)

Related work

The Generative Adversarial Networks framework has received a lot of attention lately. Despite the youth of Generative Adversarial Networks, several publications ((Arjovsky and Bottou, 2017), (Salimans et al., 2016), (Zhao et al., 2016), (Radford et al., 2015)) have investigated the use of the GAN framework for sample generation and unsupervised feature learning. Following the procedure described in (Breuleux et al., 2011) and used in (Goodfellow et al., 2014a), earlier GAN papers evaluated the quality of the fake samples by fitting a Gaussian Parzen window to the fake samples and reporting the log-likelihood of the test set under this distribution. As mentioned in (Goodfellow et al., 2014a), this method has some drawbacks, including its high variance and bad performance in high-dimensional spaces. The inception score is another widely adopted evaluation metric that fails to provide systematic guidance on the evaluation of GAN models (Barratt and Sharma, 2018).

Unlike other optimization problems, where analysis of the empirical risk is a strong indicator of progress, in GANs the decrease in loss is not always correlated with increase in image quality (Arjovsky et al., 2017), and thus authors still rely on visual inspection of generated images. Based on visual inspection, authors confirm that they have not observed mode collapse or that their framework is robust to mode collapse if some criterion is met ((Arjovsky et al., 2017), (Gulrajani et al., 2017), (Mao et al., 2016), (Radford et al., 2015)). In practice, GitHub issues, where practitioners report mode collapse or not enough variety, abound.

In their publications, Mao et al. (2016), Arjovsky et al. (2017) and Gulrajani et al. (2017) proposed alternative objective functions and algorithms that circumvent problems that are common when using the original GAN objective described in (Goodfellow et al., 2014a). The problems addressed include instability of learning, mode collapse, and meaningful loss curves (Salimans et al., 2016).

These alternatives do not eliminate the necessity of (or excitement gained from) visually inspecting GAN samples during training, nor do they provide quantitative information about the generated samples.

Feature extraction

In this section, we are going to describe and implement two features that can be used to identify GAN samples. These features include the centroid and the slope. We will briefly describe what information about images these features provide and give an implementation.

Centroid

The centroid draws inspiration from the centroid or geometric center defined in mathematics and physics, whereby it represents the arithmetic mean position of all the points in the figure. In computer vision parlance, the centroid is an image moment: a weighted average (moment) of the image pixels' intensities.

In our context, the centroid represents the arithmetic mean row in a column. For each column in an image, we transform the pixel values into row probabilities by normalizing them by the column sum, after which we take the expected row value, thus obtaining the spectral centroid. Naturally, this can be extended to include columns only or both rows and columns.

It is inspired by the spectral centroid (Peeters, 2004), a feature commonly used in the audio domain, where it represents the barycenter of the spectrum. Although this feature has been derived from the audio domain, it can be applied to other domains. The following figure shows these features computed on MNIST:

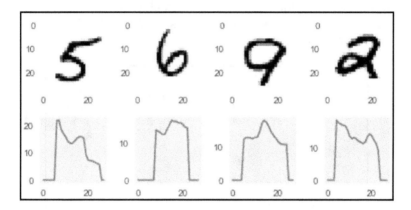

Centroid computed on numbers from the MNIST dataset

In the following code block, we describe how to compute the centroid and plot the preceding image:

```
# spectral centroid
n_samples = 4
fig, axes = plt.subplots(2, n_samples, figsize=(6, 3))

# compute centroids on n_samples
for i in range(0, n_samples):
    # randomly sample mnist_train
    img = sample('mnist_train', 1)[0, 0]

    # compute the centroids
    centroids = (np.dot(np.arange(img.shape[0]).T, img) /
                (np.sum(img, axis=0) + np.finfo(float).eps))
    # plot the images and the centroids
    axes[0, i].imshow(img)
    axes[1, i].plot(centroids)

    # use a tight layout
    plt.tight_layout()
```

Slope

The slope draws inspiration from mathematics, where it represents the steepness and direction of a line. In our context, the slope provides us with information about the overall steepness and direction of a slice of an image. It is computed by applying linear regression using an overlapping sliding window of size 7. For each window, we regress the spectral centroids on the column number mod the window size. The following figure shows these features computed on MNIST:

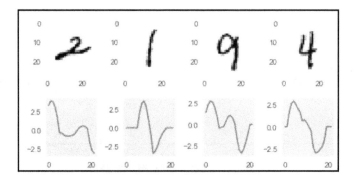

Slope computed on numbers from the MNIST dataset

The slope is also defined in the audio domain, where it is known as the spectral slope (Peeters, 2004). In the following code block, we describe how to compute the slope and plot the preceding image:

```
# spectral slope
n_samples = 4
fig, axes = plt.subplots(2, n_samples, figsize=(6, 3))

# instantiate linear model for computing the slope
lm = linear_model.LinearRegression()

# compute slope over 7 columns at a time
slope_len = 7

# compute slopes on n_samples
for i in range(0, n_samples):
    # randomly sample mnist_train
    img = sample('mnist_train', 1)[0, 0]

    # compute the centroids
    centroids = (np.dot(np.arange(img.shape[0]).T, img) /
                (np.sum(img, axis=0) + np.finfo(float).eps))
```

```
# plot the images
axes[0, i].imshow(img)

# compute the slopes frame by frame with overlap
X = np.arange(slope_len).reshape((-1, 1))
slopes = np.array([lm.fit(X, centroids[i:i+slope_len]).coef_[0]
                       for i in range(len(centroids) - slope_len + 1)])

# plot the slopes
axes[1, i].plot(slopes)

# use a tight layout
plt.tight_layout()
```

Metrics

We are going to use the **Jensen-Shannon divergence** (**JSD**)and the Kolgomorov-Smirnov Two-Sample test for comparing real samples and samples generated with GANs. We are going to use the KS Two-Sample test implementation found on `scipy.stats` and `ks_2samp`.

Jensen-Shannon divergence

As we described in `Chapter 2`, *Introduction to Generative Models*, the JSD is a symmetric and smoothed version of the Kullback-Leibler divergence:

$$JSD(P||Q) = \frac{1}{2}KL(P||M) + \frac{1}{2}KL(Q||M)$$

The implementation in Python is straightforward. First, we normally each distribution by dividing them by their respective norm such that the comparison is at the same scale. After normalizing the distributions, we compute the KL distance from P to M and Q to M, where M is the mean between the distributions P and Q:

```
from scipy.stats import entropy
from numpy.linalg import norm
def JSD(P, Q):
    # Jensen-Shannon Divergence or Symmetric KL
    _P = P / norm(P, ord=1)
    _Q = Q / norm(Q, ord=1)
    _M = 0.5 * (_P + _Q)
    return 0.5 * (entropy(_P, _M) + entropy(_Q, _M))
```

Kolgomorov-Smirnov Two-Sample test

The Kolgomorov-Smirnov Two-Sample test for comparing distributions is described as follows:

$$D_{n,m} = \sup_x |F_{1,n}(x) - F_{2,m}(x)|,$$

$F_{1,n}$ and $F_{2,m}$ are the empirical cumulative distribution functions (eCDF) of the first and the second sample respectively, and *sup* is the supremum function. The null hypothesis is rejected at level α if the following is true:

$$D_{n,m} > c(\alpha)\sqrt{\frac{n+m}{nm}}$$

Here, n and m are the sizes of the first and second sample respectively. The value of $c(\alpha)$ can be computed with the following:

$$c(\alpha) = \sqrt{-\frac{1}{2}\ln(\frac{\alpha}{2})}$$

Experiments

The experiments described in this section focus on two points: the first shows that fake samples have properties that are hardly noticed with visual inspection and that are tightly related to the requirements of differentiability; the second shows that there are numerical differences between statistical moments computed on features extracted from real and fake samples that can be used to identify the data.

MNIST

The experiment focuses on showing numerical properties of fake MNIST samples and features therein, unknown to the naked eye, which can be used to identify them as produced by a GAN. We start by comparing the distribution of features computed over the MNIST training set to other datasets, including the MNIST test set, samples generated with the **Least-Squares GAN (LSGAN)** and the **Improved Wasserstein GAN (IWGAN)**, and adversarial samples computed using the **Fast Gradient Sign Method (FGSM)**. The training data is scaled to [0, 1] and the random baseline is sampled from a Bernoulli distribution with probability equal to the mean value of pixel intensities in the MNIST training data, 0.13. Each GAN model is trained until the loss plateaus and the generated samples look similar to the real samples. The datasets we are going to compare have 10,000 samples each.

 The data can be downloaded from our GitHub repository: `https://github.com/packt/hands_on_gans_with_keras`.

The following screenshot contain the samples drawn from MNIST train, test, LSGAN, IWGAN, FSGM, and Bernoulli:

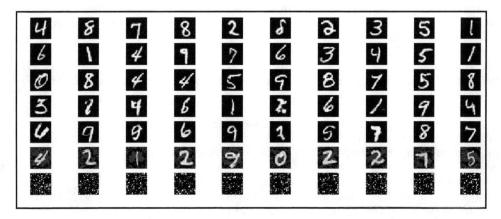

These experiments should be executed inside an IPython notebook. We start by importing the necessary libraries and packages:

```
import matplotlib
%matplotlib inline
import matplotlib.pylab as plt
import pickle as pkl
import numpy as np
from scipy.stats import moment
```

```
import statsmodels.api as sm
from sklearn import linear_model
import gzip
from scipy.stats import ks_2samp
```

We now write a helper function to load MNIST `data` that can be downloaded from Yann LeCun's website (`http://yann.lecun.com/exdb/mnist/`):

```
def load_mnist_images(filename):
    with gzip.open(filename, 'rb') as f:
        data = np.frombuffer(f.read(), np.uint8, offset=16)
    data = data.reshape(-1, 1, 28, 28)
    return data / np.float32(256)
```

Then we `load` GAN data and generate random data based on training data statistics for comparison:

```
random_size = 10000
sample_size = 1000
labels = ('mnist_train', 'mnist_test', 'mnist_train_sigmoid',
'mnist_lsgan', 'mnist_iwgan',
          'mnist_adversarial', 'random')
datasets = {}
datasets['mnist_test'] = load_mnist_images('t10k-images-idx3-ubyte.gz')
datasets['mnist_train'] = load_mnist_images('train-images-idx3-ubyte.gz'[
    :len(datasets['mnist_test'])]
datasets['mnist_adversarial'] =
pkl.load(open('MNIST_test_adversarial_010.bin', "r"))
datasets['mnist_adversarial'] = datasets['mnist_adversarial'].reshape(-1,
1, 28, 28))
datasets['mnist_lsgan'] =
np.load('lsgan_imgs.npy')[:len(datasets['mnist_test'])]
datasets['mnist_iwgan'] =
np.load('iwgan_imgs.npy')[:len(datasets['mnist_test'])]

# use the statistics of the training data to generate binomial samples
datasets['random'] = np.random.binomial(1, datasets[labels[0]].mean(),
(len(datasets['mnist_test']), 1, 28, 28))
```

Now, we are going to compute the test statistics and plot the distributions of pixel values within two ranges:

```
# we are comparing distributions on other data to the distributions on the
training data
ref = datasets[labels[0]].flatten()

# compute the empirical histogram of the reference with 100 bins and within
the [0, 1] range
```

```
ref_hist = np.histogram(ref, bins=100, range=(0.0, 1.0))[0]

fig, axes = plt.subplots(2, len(labels), figsize=(16, 4))
for i in range(len(labels)):
    tgt = datasets[labels[i]].flatten()
    # plot and compute the empirical histogram
    tgt_hist = axes[0, i].hist(tgt, bins=100, range=(0.0, 1.0))[0]
    # compute the ks 2 sample test and the jsd
    ts = ks_2samp(ref, tgt)
    jsd = JSD(ref_hist, tgt_hist)
    # plot the full distribution
    axes[0, i].set_title(labels[i])

    # plot and compute the empirical histogram on a new range
    tmin, tmax = 0.11, 0.88
    ids = (tgt > tmin) & (tgt < tmax)
    tgt_hist = axes[1, i].hist(tgt[ids], bins=100, range=(tmin, tmax))[0]
    print("{} {} JSD {}".format(labels[i], ts, jsd))

plt.tight_layout()
```

The following output shows that the GAN-generated samples smoothly approximate the modes of the distribution around 0 and 1. This smooth approximation is considerably different from the MNIST training and test sets. Although not perceptually meaningful given that the fake images seem real, these properties can be used to identify the source of the data. The distribution of pixel intensities are displayed in two ranges: [0, 1] and [0.11, 0.88]:

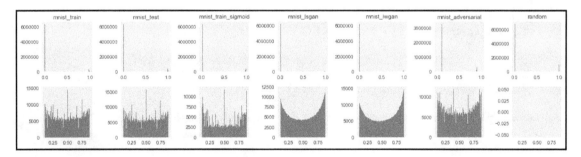

The following table shows results for KS Two-Sample test and JSD. The table reveals that although samples generated with LSGAN and IWGAN look similar to the training set, they are considerably different from the training set given by the **Kolgomorov-Smirnov (KS)** Two-Sample test and the **Jensen-Shannon Divergence (JSD)**, especially with respect to the same statistics on the MNIST test data:

	KS Two Sample Test		JSD
	Statistic	P-Value	
mnist_train	0.0	1.0	0.0
mnist_test	0.003177	0.0	0.000029
mnist_lsgan	0.808119	0.0	0.013517
mnist_iwgan	0.701573	0.0	0.014662
mnist_adversarial	0.419338	0.0	0.581769
mnist_bernoulli	0.130855	0.0	0.0785009

These numerical phenomena can be understood by investigating the empirical **cumulative distribution functions (CDF)** of pixel values. The CDF of a real-valued random variable is defined as follows:

$$F_X(x) = P(X \le x)$$

It is a function defined over the support of the random variable X that computes the probability that X will take a value that is less than or equal to x.

The following code block is used to generate the empirical CDF computed on pixel values:

```
# flatten the reference distribution
ref = datasets[labels[0]].flatten()

# create a function to compute the empirical CDF of the reference
distribution
ecdf_ref = sm.distributions.ECDF(ref)

# compute the empirical CD over 50 points evenly spaced between 0 and 1.
x = np.linspace(0, 1, num=50)
y_ref = ecdf_ref(x)

fig, axes = plt.subplots(1, len(labels), figsize=(16, 3))
axes = axes.flatten()

# iterate over the datasets
for i in range(len(labels)):
    # load the target dataset data
    tgt = datasets[labels[i]].flatten()
```

```
    # create a function to compute the empirical CDF of the target
distribution
    ecdf_tgt = sm.distributions.ECDF(tgt)
    # compute and plot the empirical CDF of the target distribution
    y = ecdf_tgt(x)
    axes[i].set_ylim((0, 1.0))
    axes[i].step(x, y_ref, colors[1])
    axes[i].step(x, y, colors[2])
    axes[i].set_title(labels[i])

plt.suptitle('Empirical CDF')
plt.tight_layout()
```

By running the code, we will obtain the following output:

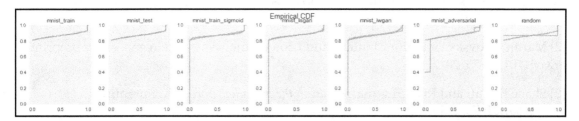

The figure shows that the distribution of pixel values of the samples generated with the GAN framework is mainly bi-modal and asymptotically approaches the modes of the distribution in the real data at 0 and 1. As expected, the FGSM method, noted as mnist_adversarial, causes a shift on the modes of the distribution that can be easily identified.

Summary

In this chapter, we investigated numerical properties of samples produced with adversarial methods, especially Generative Adversarial Networks. We showed that fake samples have properties that are barely noticed within visuals of samples, namely the fact that, due to stochastic gradient descent and the requirements of differentiability, fake samples smoothly approximate the dominating modes of the distribution. We analyzed statistical measures of divergence between real data and other data, and the results showed that even in simple cases – for instance, distribution of pixel intensities – the divergence between training data and fake data is large with respect to test data.

Although not common practice, one could possibly circumvent the difference in support between the real and fake data by training Generators that explicitly sample a distribution that replicates the support of the real data, for instance, 256 values in the case of discretized images. These are topics that are not limited to GANs and remain to be explored in the larger domain of Verified Artificial Intelligence.

In the next chapter, we will learn about latest advances in GANs.

References

[1] Martin Arjovsky and Léon Bottou. *Towards principled methods for training generative adversarial networks*. In NIPS 2016 Workshop on Adversarial Training. In review for ICLR, volume 2016, 2017.

[2] Martin Arjovsky, Soumith Chintala, and Léon Bottou. Wasserstein gan. arXiv preprint arXiv:1701.07875, 2017.

[3] Shane Barratt and Rishi Sharma. *A note on the inception score*. arXiv preprint arXiv:1801.01973, 2018.

[4] Olivier Breuleux, Yoshua Bengio, and Pascal Vincent. Quickly generating representative samples from an rbm-derived process. Neural Computation, 23(8):2058–2073, 2011.

[5] Wilson Cai, Anish Doshi, and Rafael Valle. *Attacking speaker recognition with deep generative models*. arXiv preprint arXiv:1801.02384, 2018.

[6] Ian Goodfellow, Jean Pouget-Abadie, Mehdi Mirza, Bing Xu, David Warde-Farley, Sherjil Ozair, Aaron Courville, and Yoshua Bengio. Generative adversarial nets. In Advances in neural information processing systems, pages 2672–2680, 2014.

[7] Ian J Goodfellow, Jonathon Shlens, and Christian Szegedy. *Explaining and harnessing adversarial examples*. arXiv preprint arXiv:1412.6572, 2014.

[8] Ishaan Gulrajani, Faruk Ahmed, Martin Arjovsky, Vincent Dumoulin, and Aaron Courville. *Improved training of wasserstein gans*. arXiv preprint arXiv:1704.00028, 2017.

[9] Yanick Lukic, Carlo Vogt, Oliver Dürr, and Thilo Stadelmann. Speaker identification and clustering using convolutional neural networks. In Machine Learning for Signal Processing (MLSP), 2016 IEEE 26th International Workshop on, pages 1–6. IEEE, 2016.

[10] Xudong Mao, Qing Li, Haoran Xie, Raymond YK Lau, Zhen Wang, and Stephen Paul Smolley. *Least squares generative adversarial networks*. arXiv preprint ArXiv:1611.04076, 2016.

[11] Brian McFee, Colin Raffel, Dawen Liang, Daniel PW Ellis, Matt McVicar, Eric Battenberg, and Oriol Nieto. librosa: Audio and music signal analysis in Python. In Proceedings of the 14th Python in science conference, 2015.

[12] Geoffroy Peeters. A large set of audio features for sound description (similarity and classification) in the cuidado project. Technical report, IRCAM, 2004.

[13] Alec Radford, Luke Metz, and Soumith Chintala. *Unsupervised representation learning with deep convolutional generative adversarial networks*. arXiv preprint arXiv:1511.06434, 2015.

[14] Tim Salimans, Ian J. Goodfellow, Wojciech Zaremba, Vicki Cheung, Alec Radford, and Xi Chen. Improved techniques for training gans. CoRR, abs/1606.03498, 2016.

[15] Sanjit A. Seshia and Dorsa Sadigh. Towards verified artificial intelligence. CoRR, abs/1606.08514, 2016.

[16] Junbo Zhao, Michael Mathieu, and Yann LeCun. *Energy-based generative adversarial network*. arXiv preprint arXiv:1609.03126, 2016.

12
Whats next in GANs

Now that you have been deeply exposed to deep learning and **Generative Adversarial Networks** (**GANs**), in this chapter, you will learn about the possible future avenues for GANs! We start with a summary of this book, the topics that we covered, and the knowledge that we have gained so far.

Next, we address important open questions related to GANs that are essential for interacting with GAN models. We briefly pose questions related to how important architectures are, whether GANs really learn the target distribution, whether GANs are dependent on the inductive bias of architectures, and how to identify GAN samples.

Following this, we consider the artistic use of GANs in the visual and sonic arts. In the visual arts, we provide examples of painting and video generation; while in the sonic arts, we provide examples of instrument synthesis and music generation.

Finally, we look at recent and yet-to-be-explored domains within GANs. We offer a brief discussion on **Verified Artificial Intelligence** (**Verified AI**) and explore GAN examples in biology, audio and other domains.

The following topics will be covered in this chapter:

- What we've GANed so far
- Unanswered questions in GANs
- Artistic GANs
- Recent and yet-to-be-explored GAN topics

What we've GANed so far

The GAN framework has revolutionized the fields of machine learning and deep learning. Over the course of the chapters in this book, we implemented many models in many domains that were part of this revolution, including images, text, and audio.

Generative models

We learned about deep learning and generative models in general, and their applications in AI. We covered many topics including GANs, autoregressive models, variational autoencoders, and reversible flow models.

We described in detail the building blocks of GANs, including their strengths and limitations. We learned how to visualize their results and how to evaluate them qualitatively and quantitatively.

Architectures

We learned how **Conditional GANs** (**CGANs**) work and how to implement them. We learned how to set up and train GANs, giving us the ability to control the characteristics of GAN outputs, such as the vector arithmetic in latent space.

We learned how to implement several model architectures including DCGAN, ResNet, and U-Net.

Loss functions

We learned about multiple loss functions, the problems they claim to solve, and how to implement them. We looked at the original GAN loss, the **Wasserstein GAN** (**WGAN**), the **Wasserstein GAN** with **Gradient Penalty** (**WGAN-GP**), the **Least Squares GAN** (**LSGAN**), and the **Relativistic GAN** (**RGAN**).

We also looked into adding terms to the GAN loss function, including feature matching loss, reconstruction loss, and VGG loss.

Tricks of the trade

We learned how to train GANs and circumvent the many challenges that are involved in doing so. We learned how to first identify problems with GANs and then solve them using tricks of the trade.

Implementations

We learned to implement several models in different domains. In the image domain, we implemented pix2pix, pix2pixHD, and Progressive Growing of GANs; in the text domain, we implemented natural language generation with GANs; and in the audio domain, we implemented sound enhancement GANs.

Combining the image and text domains, we implemented text-to-image synthesis. Finally, we also looked into identifying GAN samples.

We have done a lot but there still is a lot that is left to do. GANs are an ongoing field of research and there are many questions that still need to be answered! So, let's look at them.

Unanswered questions in GANs

GAN-based research is fertile and new architectures, loss functions, and tricks are being released on a daily basis. In this context of constant change, we enumerate a few questions that still need to be answered.

Are some losses better than others?

As we addressed earlier, in the paper, *Are GANs Created Equal? A Large-Scale Study*, the authors state that in their experiments, they did not find evidence that any of the tested algorithms consistently outperformed the non-saturating GAN. This leads us to wonder whether some losses are, in fact, better than others. We should bear this in mind when choosing a GAN framework.

Do GANs do distribution learning?

In their paper, *Generalization and Equilibrium in Generative Adversarial Nets (GANs)*, Sanjeev Arora et al. use the birthday paradox to suggest that GANs learn distribution with fairly low levels of support. At the same time, in their paper, *A Style-Based Generator Architecture for Generative Adversarial Networks*, Tero Karras et al. proposed that a GAN architecture is capable of generating many high-quality faces, thus suggesting that GANs have to learn a distribution with rather high levels of support. We should bear this in mind and evaluate our GANs according to the tasks that we build them for.

All about that inductive bias

In their paper *Deep Image Prior*, Dmitry Ulyanov et al. show that a randomly-initialized neural network can be used as a handcrafted prior with excellent results in standard inverse problems such as denoising, super-resolution, and inpainting. This evidence, and the evidence brought by the paper *Are GANs created Equal?*, leads us to question how important the GAN framework is with respect to the convolutional architectures that are being used to solve these problems. We should bear this in mind when developing new GAN architectures.

How can you kill a GAN?

We analyzed statistical measures of divergence between real data and other data and the results showed that even in simple cases, for example, the distribution of pixel intensities, the divergence between training data and fake data is high in comparison to the test data.

With respect to using specifications in order to train GANs, you could use specifications that are easy to learn from real data but are hardly differentiable, hence the hard-to-learn methods that rely on differentiation. We should bear in mind that specifications might not be satisfied by GANs.

Artistic GANs

In this section, we are going to explore the uses of GANs in the visual and sonic arts.

Visual arts

There are many GANs that produce impressive visual artifacts that can be used in the arts. Examples include the generation of paintings, anime characters, and fashionable clothes. Here, we provide a very small snippet of the visual work that is done using GANs.

GANGogh

GANGogh is the product of semester-long research performed by Kenny Jones and Derrick Bonafilia at Williams College in 2017.

In their project, the authors scoured the WikiArt database, which contains over 100,000 paintings, along with labels for style, genre, artist, and other features. The dataset that was used in their project contained 80,000 images with style and genre labels.

Their network setup is similar to the typical CGAN framework and is based on the improved WGAN. In the CGAN setup, the generator normally receives labels that are used to apply global conditioning on every layer; the discriminator, on the other hand, has an extra output that predicts the label of the input. In GANGogh, global conditioning was performed by applying a gated multiplicative activation function, similar to what is used in WaveNet and conditional PixelCNN.

Here are a few interesting image examples provided on their web page:

Flowers

Here is an another interesting example:

Landscapes

For more information on GANGogh, you can visit the dedicated blog at `https://towardsdatascience.com/gangogh-creating-art-with-gans-8d087d8f74a1`. Alternatively, you can find the code for GANGogh in the GitHub repository at `https://github.com/rkjones4/GANGogh`.

Image inpainting

The impactful and amazing work done by Guilin et al. on image inpainting has been featured on both Forbes and Fortune:

Image inpainting

In their paper, the authors claim that using regular convolutions for image inpainting led to issues such as color discrepancy and blurriness, and that postprocessing methods to reduce such artifacts are not efficient. Their solution to this problem is through partial convolution, in which the convolution is masked and normalized with respect to the pixels that are valid.

In the visual arts, this work represents a new avenue for exploring and synthesizing content using a smart retouching brush. GANs also played a role in the Guilin et al. image inpainting setup, and the authors used patchGAN discriminators to train the generators that are used to perform image inpainting on human faces.

For more information about image inpainting and partial convolutions, you can refer to the paper *Image Inpainting for Irregular Holes using Partial Convolutions* at `https://arxiv.org/pdf/1804.07723.pdf`. Additionally, you can visit the web page at `https://www.nvidia.com/research/inpainting/` or watch the demo at `http://masc.cs.gmu.edu/wiki/partialconv`.

Vid2Vid

Vid2Vid is an amazing technique that tackles the problem of video-to-video synthesis. Vid2Vid is an extension of the Pix2PixHD GAN, which is the same network that we implemented in this book that outperforms several state-of-the-art competing systems.

Vid2Vid was developed by Ting-Chun Wang et al. and is described in the paper, *Video-to-Video Synthesis*, published at NeurIPS in 2018. One of the most notable achievements of Vid2Vid is that it produced the first interactive AI-rendered virtual world. The following screenshot shows a person driving through this AI-rendered virtual world:

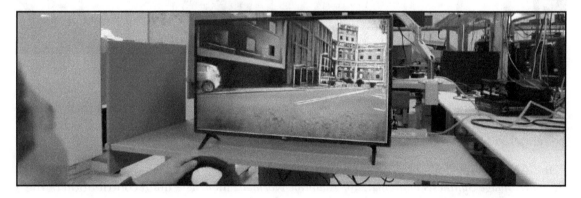

An AI-rendered virtual world

For more information about Vid2Vid, you can read the paper at `https://tcwang0509.github.io/vid2vid/`. Alternatively, you can find the code for Vid2Vid in the GitHub repository at `https://github.com/NVIDIA/vid2vid`.

GauGAN

From the creators of Pix2PixHD and Vid2VidHD, GauGAN is named after the painter Paul Gauguin. GauGAN can be referred to as a smart paintbrush that is able to transform doodles into photorealistic landscapes. Let's take a look at GauGAN in action:

The GauGAN interface

The GauGAN interface allows the user to select a type of texture or object, and then draw it by simply defining (in the left panel) the region over which the real texture or object should be rendered (in the right panel).

GauGAN was developed by Taesung Park et al. and has been published in the paper *Semantic Image Synthesis with Spatially-Adaptive Normalization*. The main contribution of the authors is the spatially-adaptive normalization, in which the affine layer that performs normalization is learned from semantic segmentation maps.

The following screenshot shows different stages of the same image conditioned on different stylizations:

A GauGAN diagram

For more information about GauGAN, you can visit the web page at `https://blogs.nvidia.com/blog/2019/03/18/gaugan-photorealistic-landscapes-nvidia-research` and the paper at `https://nvlabs.github.io/SPADE/`. Alternatively, you can find the code for GauGAN in the GitHub repository at `https://github.com/nvlabs/spade/`.

Sonic arts

Unlike the visual arts, where many GANs have been very successful in producing attractive images, the use of GANs in the sonic arts has achieved moderate success. In the following sections, we'll share some of the interesting projects in music generation and audio synthesis.

MuseGAN

The **Multitrack Sequential Generative Adversarial Network** (**MuseGAN**) was developed by Hao-Wen Dong et al. As the name suggests, MuseGAN is able to synthesize multitrack MIDI files.

MuseGAN has three GAN models for generating multitrack data:

- **The jamming model**: This consists of multiple generators that independently create a single track each.
- **The composer model**: This consists of a single generator that creates all the tracks.
- **The hybrid model**: This consists of multiple generators that are conditioned on global and individual Z vectors:

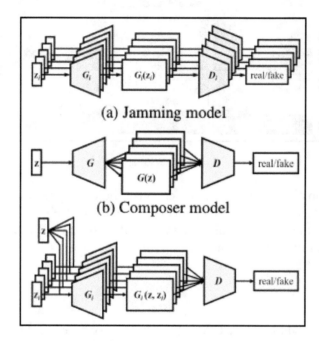

MuseGAN generator diagrams

In MuseGAN, temporal coherence is obtained by considering the following two approaches:

- **Generation from scratch**: Here, a temporal structure generator and a bar generator are used.
- **Track-conditional generation**: Here, the generator takes a conditioning input.

For more information about MuseGAN, you can visit the web page at `https://salu133445.github.io/musegan/`. Alternatively, you can find the code for MuseGAN in the GitHub repository at `https://github.com/salu133445/musegan`.

GANSynth

GANSynth was developed by Google's Magenta group. GANSynth is a model for audio synthesis using GANs that are trained on the NSynth dataset.

Similar to WaveGlow, GANSynth can generate audio considerably faster than its autoregressive counterparts because it can generate an entire sequence in parallel.

Another interesting feature of GANSynth is that it enables interpolation in timbre space.

For more information about GANSynth, you can visit the web page at `https://storage.googleapis.com/magentadata/papers/gansynth/index.html`. Alternatively, you can find the code for GANSynth at `https://github.com/tensorflow/magenta/tree/master/magenta/models/gansynth`.

Recent and yet-to-be-explored GAN topics

In this section, we will cover a few recent and yet-to-be-explored topics of GANs that are challenging, interesting, and valuable.

In my opinion, one of the most interesting topics in GANs and deep learning is verified AI. This topic was described in Sanjit Seshia's *Towards Verified AI* paper in 2016 and is later addressed in a blog post by Google's DeepMind team. There are many challenges involved in achieving verified AI. Some of these challenges include testing, training, and formally proving that the models are specification-consistent.

Other fields that have recently received attention from GAN researchers include biology and its related subfields. There are GAN models that address the problem of drug discovery (*3D Molecular Representations Based on the Wave Transform for Convolutional Neural Networks*) and real-valued time series generation (*Real-valued (Medical) Time Series Generation with Recurrent Conditional GANs*).

Audio synthesis is a topic that has also received some attention in the GAN community. GANSynth and WaveGAN are GAN models that have been used for audio synthesis. Chris Donahue's has an interesting demo website that uses WaveGAN to fuel a drum loop at `https://chrisdonahue.com/wavegan/`.

There are many other tasks in which GANs have been used, such as in the estimation of individualized treatment effects (GANITE), multivariate time-series imputation (*Multivariate Time Series Imputation with Generative Adversarial Networks*), and autonomous driving (D-GAN, DeepRoad, and SADGAN), and more.

Summary

In this chapter, we learned about the recent advances of GANs. We started with a summary of this book and expanded our knowledge from the simplest GAN framework to state-of-the-art GANs. We then addressed a few important open questions related to GANs. We then considered the artistic uses of GANs in the visual and sonic arts. Finally, we briefly explored new and yet-to-be-explored domains within GANs.

Closing remarks

By now, you should have acquired a broad understanding of deep learning and a deep understanding of the GAN framework. We are confident, that by now, you are able to use the GAN framework to train your own state-of-the-art models for several tasks and domains. We look forward to seeing your models being shared on GitHub and deployed in real life.

Join the revolution, seek adversarial relationships, and collaborate with the future of GANs because: yes, we GAN!

Further reading

An extensive list of GAN models, also known as GAN Zoo, and further reading can be found at the following URLs:

- Minchul Shin has a deep list of GANs and their applications on his GitHub page at `https://github.com/nashory/gans-awesome-applications`.
- Avinash Hindupuer has a deep alphabetic list of GANs on his GitHub page at `https://github.com/hindupuravinash/the-gan-zoo`.

Other Books You May Enjoy

If you enjoyed this book, you may be interested in these other books by Packt:

Generative Adversarial Networks Cookbook
Josh Kalin

ISBN: 9781789139907

- Structure a GAN architecture in pseudocode
- Understand the common architecture for each of the GAN models you will build
- Implement different GAN architectures in TensorFlow and Keras
- Use different datasets to enable neural network functionality in GAN models
- Combine different GAN models and learn how to fine-tune them
- Produce a model that can take 2D images and produce 3D models
- Develop a GAN to do style transfer with Pix2Pix

Generative Adversarial Networks Projects
Kailash Ahirwar

ISBN: 9781789136678

- Train a network on the 3D ShapeNet dataset to generate realistic shapes
- Generate anime characters using the Keras implementation of DCGAN
- Implement an SRGAN network to generate high-resolution images
- Train Age-cGAN on Wiki-Cropped images to improve face verification
- Use Conditional GANs for image-to-image translation
- Understand the generator and discriminator implementations of StackGAN in Keras

Leave a review - let other readers know what you think

Please share your thoughts on this book with others by leaving a review on the site that you bought it from. If you purchased the book from Amazon, please leave us an honest review on this book's Amazon page. This is vital so that other potential readers can see and use your unbiased opinion to make purchasing decisions, we can understand what our customers think about our products, and our authors can see your feedback on the title that they have worked with Packt to create. It will only take a few minutes of your time, but is valuable to other potential customers, our authors, and Packt. Thank you!

Index